The 60-Second Referral
for Small Business Owners
& Independent Professionals

The 60-Second Referral
for Small Business Owners
& Independent Professionals

**9 Simple Ways to Build Relationships –
and Win the Hearts, Minds and Referrals
of Your Contacts in Only 60 Seconds a Day**

Anita Williams

Iffic Publishing Company
Winnsboro, Texas

Published by Iffic Publishing Company
800 W. Coke Road
Winnsboro, TX 75494
903-342-0022

ISBN print edition 1-4392-4283-6

Printed in the United States of America

Library of Congress Cataloging-in-Publication Data

Williams, Anita

The 60-Second Referral
for Small Business Owners & Independent Professionals
9 Simple Ways to Build Relationships –
and Win the Hearts, Minds and Referrals
of Your Contacts in Only 60 Seconds a Day

Includes References, Sources and Index

TABLE OF CONTENTS

> *"No matter how artful or talented you are, you must follow a specific methodology to be successful in expecting and getting quality referrals."*
>
> Scott Kramnick

FOREWORD

What is the secret to generating all the referrals you can handle? I'm often asked this question by small business owners and independent professionals. My answer is simple: Friends refer friends. So if you want to generate more referrals, get more friends!

Think about it. People usually respect, trust, and have positive feelings about their friends, and so they tend to talk about them to others. In fact, all things being equal, people will usually refer a friend over an even more qualified professional.

Here are three reasons why it makes sense to take the time and resources to make more friends.

First, people who were referred by a friend tend to refer more often themselves.

Second, referrals from friends tend to spend more money and spend it more often.

And third, referrals from friends are typically much more loyal and profitable, especially since there aren't any acquisition costs involved in getting them as client.

In Stephen Covey's groundbreaking book, *The 7 Habits of Highly Effective People,* he talks about the concept of an "emotional bank account." The concept states that each of us has individual internal emotional bank accounts with those people (or companies) with whom we have relationships. And just as with any bank account, you can either make deposits or withdrawals.

But instead of dealing with monetary value, we deal with emotional units. The more positive emotional units you deposit into a person's bank account, the better friends you become and the more they will refer you and your business.

The best way to create an emotional unit (and better friendships) is through simple, down-to-earth communications. The more you communicate with people in a positive, uplifting and valuable way, the better your friendship becomes.

This book teaches you nine specific ways to make daily deposits of positive emotional units through simple communications into your prospect's or customer's emotional bank account. The more times you make a deposit, the better friends you become and the more referrals you receive.

For instance, how do you feel about a person (or company) that says "thank you," or sends you information they know you're interested in, or that actually apologizes to you when they make a mistake? That's the type of person you want to tell others about, and that person can be YOU.

There's only one problem. If you asked most business owners if staying in touch with and befriending their prospects and customers is important, 100% of them would say, "Of course!" But if you then asked them if they were actually doing it, most would be embarrassed to say that they weren't.

The reason that I most commonly hear from business owners as to why they don't do more befriending is that they don't have the time, know-how or staff to keep track of and stay in touch, on a personal basis, with their prospects and customers. I hear comments like, "I know I should be reaching out to my customers, but I just don't have the time," or "We want to touch our customers more often but we don't have the staff." Although these are valid concerns, they should not be a roadblock to doing these critically important activities.

But that's where *The 60-Second Referral* comes in. In this book you'll discover the exact touch points at which you should contact a person, what to say to them, and most importantly, a repeatable, automated system for putting those processes on near autopilot.

The 60-Second Referral hits the nail on the head when it introduces the concept of the "Perpetual Contact System™." This is the secret key to creating a never-ending stream of referrals from your prospects and customers, and it's what's missing in 99% of all businesses today.

I suggest you study this book by reading it several times. Then give it to all your "friends" whom you care about and want to succeed.

David Frey
Author, *The Small Business Marketing Bible*
Founder, www.MarketingBestPractices.com

CHAPTER 1

How You Can Build Solid Relationships that Increase Sales, Loyalty and Referrals (and Why It's So Easy!)

Be well, do good work, and keep in touch.
Garrison Keeler

This book is written especially for. . .

▸ Small business owners, including retailers, restaurant owners, and other types of brick and mortar companies.

▸ Professionals in private practice, including doctors and other health practitioners, lawyers, accountants, consultants and coaches.

▸ Service providers, including independent contractors and the trades.

▸ Home-based business owners in all fields.

Best-selling author Michael Port sums up the problem for small businesses, service providers and professionals. . .

"The lack of a solid keep-in-touch marketing strategy is where most businesses fail. Either they bombard you with too much information and too many offers that turn you off, or you never hear from them at all, which leaves you feeling unimportant and irrelevant."

You'll learn that marketing isn't the only valid reason to stay in touch, and customers aren't the only people who deserve your attention. If you know you need to take better care of your clients, customers and prospects – as well as business associates, friends, family and even acquaintances – you're not alone.

If you also know that all-important referrals start with trust and a real connection with people, this book is pure gold for you.

Why? Because having contacts isn't enough. Building relationships is the key. This concept is lost on many who simply have contacts, but no real connection with people.

So what's stopping you?

Here are the five roadblocks that stand between you and building successful relationships.

Most small business owners, professionals in private practice, and independent contractors squander their opportunities to build real relationships that can enhance their businesses and their lives. In business, relationships build loyalty. . . and referrals.

See if one or more of the following apply to you. . .

1. **You haven't made cultivating relationships a priority.** You aren't alone. For all the seminars, books and coaching to "stay in touch" with prospects, customers and even business colleagues, hardly anyone does it on a regular, consistent basis.

   For some, it's not important. They're focused on quick sales. Others know it's important, but never get started or contact people on a hit-and-miss basis.

   Terrie Williams, a PR specialist who owns The Terrie Williams Agency, wrote about many ways to enhance relationships in *The Personal Touch* (1996).

   "The fact of the matter is, most people don't do these things. So when you do, you stand out. . . Understand that your relationship with people. . . has as much to do with your success as all your professional knowledge – maybe even more."

2. **You don't have time** to stay in touch with a large number of people on a continuing basis. You may be overloaded already and assume an effective system will take a lot of your limited time.

Does your business rely on referrals? Repeat business? Joe Girard sold more cars one-on-one for 12 consecutive years than anyone else. And he made it into the *Guinness Book of World Records.*

He collected contact and personal information on every prospect and every customer and stayed in touch with them by mail once a month. That was a total of 13,000 greeting cards every month, a feat made possible with the help of two assistants.

Obviously, you'll scale your contact strategy to what is appropriate for your business. Fortunately, technology can automate the process, but this is the point. . .

Joe's success was based on *consistency* and *friendly, lighthearted messages.*

3. **You don't know how to keep in touch regularly**. Many small business owners, professionals and service providers stay in touch with active customers, but only when it applies directly to the work.

   If it's a plan you need, you'll discover several simple strategies in this book. There is no single "right" way to keep in touch.

   In this book we refer to a **Perpetual Contact System**™. That's simply our term for the **technology** that works for you, **combined with the messages** you use to keep in touch.

4. **You don't have a simple system to implement continuous communications**. Once you have a plan, you need a delivery system. If you're technologically challenged, you'll be glad to know there are low-tech solutions outlined in this book that you can use.

5. **You don't know what to say.** Most people don't consider themselves great writers. They can e-mail or text a quick message, but faced with sending an apology or a thank-you note, they're stumped.

The timely note that should be sent today is postponed until tomorrow. . . then next week. . . and often doesn't get sent at all.

You'll find out here that you're better prepared than you think.

If any of these five apply to you, this book will let you remove the roadblocks and start building relationships that will change your business – and life – for the better. The path between good relationships and referrals is short and direct.

Just having names in a file and proficiency in your field isn't enough. . .

Ellin Sanger, a celebrity booker and TV producer, says, "You can have a great Rolodex and know the mechanics of booking. But that's not enough. In the end, it's all about relationships."

In this book, you'll discover how to do one simple task that takes 60-seconds a day to turn contacts into relationships and relationships into referrals.

Let's get started with some basic orientation in Chapter 2 – The Value of Building and Maintaining Relationships.

Note to readers:

Lew Williams is my husband and business partner. Although he is not a co-author of this book, he was deeply involved in its development. Throughout the book, when you read "we" or "us," it refers to us as a team and our joint experience.

Also, there are numerous stories in the book. These present representative examples, but include fictionalized information and composite characters to conceal identities and streamline the stories.

CHAPTER 2

The Value of Building and Maintaining Relationships

When you get right down to it. . . it is how you connect with people on a human personal level that will ensure your success. Relationships are key.

Terrie Williams, author, *The Personal Touch,* 1996

In this Chapter. . .

▸ What technology can and can't do to help build your relationships.

▸ Why consultants and independent contractors have a real advantage over larger competitors.

▸ How to cut through the clutter and information overload to get your message through.

▸ The key to building a strong, cordial network of real relationships.

Paul was overwhelmed. As an independent human resources consultant, he always had **too much to do** and **too little time** to do it. He had great intentions of contacting the people who were entered into his database. But weeks and months went by and he never got around to it.

When he heard about a seminar to help small businesses owners "leverage" their lists, he signed up. Although there were a few good tips, the primary purpose of the seminar was to encourage attendees to buy a new software program to sell more efficiently.

Paul didn't need new software. He needed to know **when to contact people** and **what to send them** that wasn't always a blatant sales pitch. He needed to know how to cultivate people in a way that would prompt referrals automatically, as consultants routinely rely on referrals to generate new business.

Can you relate to Paul's dilemma? Whether you're a consultant, service provider, independent contractor or retailer, or you own some other type of small business, you're in the people business. That means **you're in the relationship business.**

Names and addresses that sit ignored in a database – or worse, in drawers, address books, pockets and the basket where you keep loose change – is not a network. **Consistently cultivating** those people, along with new people you meet from now on, is what makes your list important.

Without meaningful contact, networks are not very useful for you personally or for your business. But when you stay in touch, your passive list of contacts comes alive. It has warmth, life and. . . potential. Staying top-of-mind means repeat sales. Good relationships prompt strong referrals.

Consultants and other independent contractors face common challenges when trying to figure out how to build relationships.

The following challenges may be as true for you as they are for others. . .

- ▶ **No time** and **small budget.**

- ▶ Not knowing **who** to stay in touch with. . . **or why.**

- ▶ **Believing** that staying in touch is only to build **relationships** that ultimately **result in a sale.**

- ▶ Lack of **a simple system** to stay in touch.

And one more common mistake that many independent professionals and service providers make. . .

- ▶ **Assuming that technology alone is the key** to building relationships.

With technology, the logistics of keeping in touch are much easier and the costs are lower. But don't be fooled. . .

**Technology is not the key to successful relationships.
Your personal touch – the *message* – is the key.**

This is a somewhat radical statement in today's Internet-based, multi-tasked, hyper-tech world. Please let me explain.

Today we have **unprecedented connectivity**, but **we aren't really connected**. The personal touch has been lost.

Despite our hyper-connectivity, it's tough to get connected with people. And once you reach them, it's equally tough to get and keep their attention for more than a nano-second.

That applies to TV spots, magazine ads, yellow pages, radio spots, billboards, a sign on the side of a bus, the ads flashing at you while looking at the headlines on a news site. . . and on and on.

People are burdened with such incredible **information overload**, it's hard to capture anyone's attention for any reason. This is true even if it's a topic of interest to a reader or viewer.

Twitter, e-mail and text messaging from "friends" you have never met can generate a lot of contact, but they are frequently superficial, not meaningful, connections.

The **promise** of all communications technology has always been ever-increasing, more efficient connectivity. But all that technology has only one basic **purpose**: *to deliver a message. . . a message that is on target for the recipient.*

And the reason for the targeted message is to provide value to the recipient. Adding value to another person's life is the glue that helps us bond with others.

How do you get through to people who are allegedly in your network in a way that they'll pay attention and even be grateful to hear from you?

In this book, you'll learn how to **break through the clutter of information with personal messages** that will **capture the attention** of the recipient and **strengthen the relationship**.

~~~~~~

Seth Godin asks, "What if you could turn clutter into an asset?" (*Permission Marketing*, 1999)

~~~~~~

You can do just that. And this book will show you how.

Why is this important? It's simple. Small businesses can't rely on advertising alone to attract and keep customers. Consultants, independent professionals and service providers build strong businesses primarily through relationships, not advertising.

You are naturally better equipped to cut through the clutter, as you'll learn throughout this book.

First, let's look at the four key reasons why technology in itself is not key to successful relationships. . .

1. **E-mail** – Unless you're corresponding directly with a client or customer via e-mail about a project, your message may be ignored or filed unopened.

   If you've ever filed an "interesting" e-mail to read later, you know filing is essentially the same as deleting. The likelihood of the message ever being read is almost zero. The intended communication is lost.

   Without a meaningful message that reaches and is read by the recipient, e-mail is not a reliable point of contact.

2. **Social networking** – Twitter and social networking sites, such as Facebook, are proving to be effective points of contact with customers by letting them get to know you and feel a certain level of familiarity and inclusion in "your" group.

   From a marketing standpoint, you can get news and links in front of many people by sliding right by the backlog of e-mail in their In boxes. But there's a limit to how much one-to-one contact you'll have through these methods.

3. **Contact management software** – There are many software programs designed to help the small business or practice automate correspondence, both online or off-line.

It's very common for people to input contact information into CRM software and never follow up. From our experience with small business owners and professionals, many don't know when to make contact or what to say.

Marketing gurus promote the use of such software exclusively to sell. Few explain how to build and maintain relationships using contact management software.

Obviously, we're 100% for selling; we're direct response marketing specialists. However, to make every contact a sales pitch conveys the message that you're self-serving, with little interest in your customers or clients.

4. **Web sites** – Many Web sites of small business owners, service providers and professionals are passive online brochures. A percentage of these sites use the interactive power of the Internet to strike up a conversation with people. However, most companies follow up with a short series of sales messages, and little else.

Think of **technology as the delivery system**. This can include managing the lists, tracking results and crunching the numbers, but at its core, technology is the "how" of communicating with prospects and customers. **Messages are the deliverable**: the "what."

There are any number of analogies that illustrate this point. Phone lines are the delivery system; calls are the deliverable. UPS is the delivery system; packages are the deliverable.

The failure of technology to deliver on the promise of creating real connections is based on a major misunderstanding, one that's invisible to many so-called "experts." This insight alone can transform how you interact with everyone in your world, from clients or customers and colleagues to friends and family.

There are **two primary ways people interact** with companies and individuals.

Transactional **interactions are focused on sales and profits**. This is the default interaction method of most companies with their clients and customers.

For example, you see something you want on a Web site. You buy. The purchase prompts a "thank you" page with a receipt. Your digital product is delivered online as a download. Or merchandise is delivered to your door.

Further contacts from that business, though friendly, are usually designed to sell more products. If the company can determine through its records what your purchasing patterns are, they can save you time (and increase their advertising ROI) by offering you items you're likely to buy.

Of course, there is nothing inherently wrong with a transactional relationship, but it's based on trading something for something.

A good example of a successful transactional relationship is between Amazon and its repeat buyers. Most of us who make Amazon our first stop when shopping for books, for example, come back because the site "knows" the topics and authors we like and makes suggestions based on our preferences. Of course, there are video downloads and a vast array of products as well.

Plus with 1-Click convenience, you can make a purchase with a single keystroke. What's not to love? It's a shopping paradise.

However, actually talking to a live human being at Amazon has always been a challenge.

Amazon's brainy technology is efficient and useful to customers, but that doesn't qualify as a relationship. The human touch shows up in the customer reviews and feedback, which are not from the company.

Relational **interactions can include, but go beyond, the transactional level**. This is one-on-one contact built on a human scale with human values. Interaction, loyalty and referrals live in this arena, not the transactional arena.

This is where you can shine in ways your larger competitors simply can't, even if you work alone. The reason is simple. While **large companies can simulate a relationship, you can actually have one** with the people in your entire network, not just customers.

The purpose of this book is to show you why and how to do this easily, without being overwhelmed.

For the moment, let's focus on the customer relationship because it's a major concern of most small business owners and independent professionals.

We've all received personalized letters from stores, banks, insurance companies, credit card companies and charities. Personalization generally works better in direct mail than non-personalized mail, which is the only reason they bother to spend the money to personalize.

Nevertheless, getting your name spelled correctly on an automated letter does not amount to a relationship.

As you know, even when you receive a mailing from a company you do business with, much of the "just for you" information is drawn from the information they have about you in their Customer Relationship Management (CRM) database.

If a company hasn't captured you as a customer yet, there are data companies that can tell them more about you than your own family knows so they can speak to you more "personally."

All of this targeting, from a strictly business standpoint, makes perfect sense because they're focused on Return on Investment – ROI. However, their customers become *objects* whose only value is to spend more with the company.

As effective as all this targeting is, there's a fundamental flaw in Customer Relationship Management as it is often taught and implemented today.

Companies don't manage the customer. The relationship is completely at the discretion of the client or customer. In reality. . .

The customer manages the relationship.

The consumer says, "I'll have a conversation with you; it will be all on my terms."

Jeff Swartz, CEO Timberland,
Fast Company, September, 2008

Google "CRM" and you'll find over 80 million entries, most of which are all about technology. Little wonder even small business owners think of customer contact as a technical issue, not a human one.

This fosters a somewhat cold and cynical view that customers can somehow be "managed." This premise is taught by at least two leading authorities, and subscribed to by many businesses.

Their credo is summarized in this cryptic statement: "Products are administered. Customers are managed."

Where's the humanity in that? The warmth? Dare we say it, the *human connection*?

Embed this in your mind right now: today the customer manages the relationship. Period.

As direct marketing professionals, my husband and business partner, Lew, and I have deep experience in utilizing the dissected information to create meaningful sales messages that are well received by customers.

Nevertheless, most large corporations are more company- and product-centric, not customer-centric. It's the "numbers game" model that works at that scale. But while the messages are personalized, they rarely feel personal.

Thomas Peters and Robert Waterman in their book, *In Search of Excellence,* found that successful companies were those that had a heart. These companies connect through emotion."

You, as a small business owner, can design your company to be more human-scaled and have a heart. That means. . .

You can create real relationships that generate good will, referrals and, ultimately, sales.

In short, you can do what your larger competitors can't do effectively. You can build a personal, one-on-one bond with prospects, customers, vendors and associates.

We have a tendency to think that interactions in business are entirely different than those with social contacts, including family, friends and acquaintances.

That's simply not true.

Perhaps you've been struggling to come up with "business" communications. You may be frustrated because. . .

You aren't, and **never have been, comfortable "selling,"** even though you know that to succeed, people must buy your products or services.

You feel somewhat **intimidated when you have to write** a business communication.

No one has ever shown you **how to build relationships** with regular letters, notes, cards or other communications.

You know the importance of referrals for building your business, but have no idea how to go about getting them.

As you continue through the book, you'll see how easy it is to overcome these hindrances. You'll discover how to turn your dormant list into a powerful network that will enhance your business *and* your life because. . .

Customers are important, but so are others in your business and life.

This is where you, as an independent professional, service provider or small business owner, have an edge. The reason is that you routinely communicate one-on-one.

And while large companies try to simulate relationships, no matter whose name is at the bottom of the letter, the recipient is still a "buying unit" or a "select" in a particular "market sector."

In your business, it's different. You have many people in your life. The lines between business and social relationships are quite likely to be blurred.

One of the best reasons to stay in touch with people in all areas of your life – business and social – is simple. . . to strengthen and deepen those relationships.

Why would you do this? Because it enriches your life in ways you can't anticipate.

"But shouldn't I be focusing on marketing? Don't I stay in touch so I can market to people?"

I'm so glad you asked. This is a key point.

> David Rippe and Jared Rosen explore a trend to a more sane, humane and human-scaled culture in their book, *The Flip* (2006).
>
> In the chapter about corporations they write, "Just as the newborn inherits the traits and characteristics of its parents based on genetics, environment and guidance, so does a company take on the traits and characteristics of its founders. . .
>
> "A company also has a corporate culture defined by the attitudes and actions of its current leaders."

What is true at the corporate level is equally true for your solo practice or small business venture. And you are the leader. That means you not only *can*, but automatically *will* bring to bear your traits and attitudes in your business.

What a relief. You can be a person – a human – as you do business. If you're shy and work alone because you aren't a people-person, you can still learn to build relationships without having a complete personality makeover.

You won't have to struggle to figure out how to ask for referrals from people you barely know. That's embarrassing and awkward.

People who know and trust you will have no problem dropping your name to people they know.

An overwhelming number of people teaching business-to-business marketing today talk a good story when it comes to relationship building, but often fail to make an important distinction.

There's a huge difference between a thinly veiled sales pitch and a message intended to be of interest or benefit to the recipient and/or to make them feel good.

But more importantly, many gurus teach that the people who don't spend money with you don't even deserve to be on your radar. They're a waste of time and money. We disagree. You'll find out why in Chapter 3.

Summary. . .

▸ Effective contact is dependent on the message.

▸ Your personal message can break through the clutter when you send actual mail.

▸ Most companies strive for an effective transactional relationship tied to profits alone. You can succeed with a relational focus tied to human values.

▸ Building relationships extends beyond customers or clients and prospects.

> "... If you don't take the time to establish credibility, you're not going to get the referral. People have to get to know you. They have to feel comfortable with who you are and what you do."
>
> Ivan Misner

CHAPTER 3

Your Five Relationship Circles

Only connect.

E. M. Forster, *Howards End*

In this Chapter. . .

▶ Why staying in touch is vital to your business and your life.

▶ Why all five circles of relationship are important.

▶ Why it's important to cultivate acquaintances.

▶ Why courting your prospects and romancing your customers is a better approach than typical sales tactics alone.

▶ How nine common human interactions can be used to develop successful and satisfying business and personal relationships.

Penny, a nutritional coach who ran a busy private practice, looked at her calendar and realized she'd forgotten her nephew's birthday. Again. She made a note to send him a card.

Her extended family was spread across the country and she didn't get to see them often. Unfortunately, she missed so many birthdays and anniversaries, her family had come to believe that for Penny, business came first.

She glanced at her to-do list and saw that she still hadn't sent a thank-you note to John, her friend and accountant, for the lavish lunch to celebrate her third anniversary in business. Right under that reminder was a list of prospects she needed to contact.

Face-to-face, Penny connected well with her clients. Yet the nature of her specialty meant that clients tended to drop out once they saw even modest improvements in their health. That was one of the things she and John had discussed over lunch.

He'd tracked how long people stayed in the program. The average length of time people worked with her was nine weeks. He gently suggested that she keep in contact with her former clients because most would need help again and might not come back without a nudge.

But when? How? If she couldn't even get a birthday card to her nephew, how could she manage contacting dozens of past clients?

Penny felt increasingly isolated herself. How could she possibly add anything else to her overloaded schedule?

◆ ◆ ◆

Real relationships are built on a foundation of strong human, and even spiritual, values.

In this chapter, we explore the different types of business and personal relationships you have. This includes close friends to casual acquaintances. You'll see why it's important to stay in touch with all of them.

You have five key circles of relationships. . .

1. **Customers or clients** – individuals within companies who've paid you money for your goods or services.

2. **Prospects** – the people who've indicated they're potential users of your products or services, or those you believe would be interested.

3. **Business associates** – your peers, suppliers, previous co-workers, ex-bosses, or anyone who shows up regularly in your business life who isn't a customer or client.

4. **Friends & family** – the people you rely on and who rely on you.

5. **Acquaintances** – people you just met while traveling or at social or business events, the friendly faces at church, school or around town.

When you start paying attention to individuals in all these groups, a number of really important things can occur, and making a sale is only one positive outcome.

Let's look at the pay-off of staying in touch with each of these five groups.

Romance your customers and clients.

How many times have you heard "You wouldn't expect to propose to someone on the first date"?

In reality, the whole marriage analogy is off the mark. Your customers never "marry" you. Customers are polygamous.

Just because someone enjoys having a leisurely latte at Barnes & Noble while checking out the new best sellers on a Saturday afternoon doesn't mean she isn't also ordering books at Amazon Sunday morning.

In the same way, your customers can be loyal to you, but also be loyal to other companies like yours.

The notion that once a person becomes a customer, they "belong" to you is a marketing ideal, a myth, not reality. Even experts in the field of customer loyalty will tell you **customers are more fickle now than ever**. This is true with name-brand products as well as retailers.

An article in *Ivey Business Journal* reports, "Interestingly, consumer behavior theorists have coined new terms to describe this new situation.

"'Choice repertoire' identifies the fact that a consumer can no longer be identified by a brand, but rather by a set of brands he or she will choose. . . within the same product category."

("The Roots of Brand Loyalty Decline," March 2005)

In today's marketplace – whether you serve consumers or businesses – you have to open your eyes and see that **winning customers is an ongoing process**. And that customer satisfaction is not an indicator of loyalty.

Jeffrey Gitomer pounds that idea home in his classic book, *Customer Satisfaction is Worthless. Customer Loyalty is Priceless,* released first in 1998 and still a best-seller.

A satisfied customer, according to Gitomer, ". . . felt OK about dealing with you. Their needs were met. The product was OK. The service was OK. The experience was OK. They are satisfied with their purchase. . ."

On the other hand, a loyal customer, ". . . feels GREAT about dealing with you. Their needs were met and/or exceeded. Your delivery was GREAT. The experience was GREAT. They are ecstatic. . . will proactively talk about the experience. . . refer someone. . . WOW!"

"Romancing your customer" is a different lens to use when looking at your relationship with those who buy your products or services. In real life, if you want a relationship to grow, you never abandon romance. Your primary focus is on the other person, not your own self-interest.

Ironically, when you keep the customer's interests first, you don't have to beg for referrals. They will be given freely. On the other hand, the customer who feels unimportant (or valuable only as a referral source, that is, a means to an end) will steadfastly resist any effort to generate new business for you.

To keep this concept front and center in our clients' minds, we coined the phrase **Romancing My Customer**™ – RMC: the heart of CRM. This idea turns CRM inside out and gives you a new context for your customer contacts and puts the emphasis on the "relationship" first.

Romance, above all, is making the other person feel cared for and valued. It hints at the fact that the customer should be treated in a way that fosters an **emotional connection**, which goes beyond reason or logic.

It transforms the typical *transactional* approach into a *relational* approach. And because you're a small business owner or independent professional, it's a natural expression of your human values.

Court your prospects.

Most of your prospects, including referrals, are likely to be strangers to you.

Seth Godin addressed the issue when he wrote, "Today, most marketers don't notice, or interact with people until they are customers. Some don't even pay close attention until the consumer becomes a loyal customer. . .

". . . They need to have a process in place that nurtures total strangers from the moment they first indicate interest.

"At that moment, a suite of marketing messages must begin to be applied." (*Permission Marketing*, 1999)

Lew and I agree with this, but also contend that all the messages should *not* be sales pitches. Relationship-building messages with instruction, insider information, and individual notes to the prospect should be in the mix.

Let's assume you have a Web site where visitors who are even vaguely interested in what you have to offer can opt in to your list. This may be a strong signal that they're interested in what you have to offer, or they may be only mildly interested and just want your free e-book, audio seminar or whatever you offer in exchange for limited contact information.

Because you want to sell something, the follow-ups are designed to move the prospect to the sale. Nevertheless, if every autoresponder you send is a hard-sell pitch, the prospects often back off.

We help our clients with this all-important conversion challenge. And there's only one sane way to approach it: You must look at the process from the prospect's point of view. What do they want now? What information would most prospects want to see next?

If your focus is on providing what the prospect is looking for, you can move them to a sale, or to the realization your product or service isn't for them. Knowing who isn't interested is as important as identifying those who are.

Often, inexperienced online marketers expect to go from first "hello" to sale in one step. That happens, according to a number of sources, only about one percent of the time.

Here are the reasons people don't buy instantly. . .

‣ Their **buying cycle doesn't match your sales cycle**. If they're just doing research on a product or service, but don't need it right now, nothing you do is likely to speed up the process.

‣ Once they get whatever you're offering in exchange for their name and contact information, they discover **what you're offering isn't quite what they expected** after all. They are not really prospects despite opting into your list.

‣ They discover your product or service is what they want, but the **price point is too high** or comes with more bells and whistles than they really need.

The Goldilocks theory works here. Consider offering your products or services in "Mama, Papa and Baby" sizes so the prospect can find one that's "just right" for their needs.

‣ **They're ignoring your e-mails**. On a scale of 1-10, their interest in your product or service was a 2. They aren't eagerly waiting for your next pitch to hit their In box.

One powerful way to cut **through the clutter is to include off-line contacts**. The percentage of "real" mail – not bills, not catalogs, not credit card offers – is very small.

A special occasion card – or even a personalized post card – can make a big impression.

Even so, how long do you cultivate prospects? It depends on your product or service and the life-time value of a customer in your business. It also depends on your business model.

People who market online exclusively can economically continue sending e-mails indefinitely until the prospect becomes a customer or opts out of the list. However, be aware that e-mail open rates and response rates continue to fall.

If you're a consultant or independent contractor, you may know that building a relationship is necessary before a prospect will be willing to consider hiring you. In that case, regular mailings, white papers and personal contacts could go on for months.

The key is that you technically may be communicating business to business, but in reality, it's the **personal relationship built one-to-one** that's necessary to secure assignments.

If you own a store or restaurant, on the other hand, your strategy may be to get prospects into your establishment through off-line mailings or ads with a special offer. Then you begin a concentrated effort to turn them into regular customers with ongoing contacts, both online and off-line.

No matter what your strategy, a Perpetual Contact System is essential. Personal communications can make a difference in building the relationship, which, in turn, builds trust.

Bond with business associates.

We all have associates who are part of our everyday business life. It's not unusual to have associates we've known for decades because we're in the same industry. Others own companies or work at vendors we've dealt with for years.

This is probably true for everyone who is self-employed. If you were employed in the past, this would include your co-workers, people in other departments and even subordinates or bosses.

These are often **cordial, but not close, relationships**. Nevertheless, because of the continued contact, we become quite friendly.

Candidly, these relationships are often limited to time, location and circumstance. Typically, once you're no longer working together or running into each other at the same events, the relationships simply evaporate. Yet it doesn't have to be that way.

Fortunately, today you can reconnect with old school mates, co-workers and friends through LinkedIn, Plaxo, Facebook and other networking sites, or simple "people search" options using the White Pages sites online.

Among the many people you work with in the course of business, there are those who make an impression: A supplier who goes the extra mile to make sure you get all your materials for a trade show in spite of a tight deadline. A client's accountant who expedites your invoice so you're paid on time.

If you didn't become best buddies when work put you in the same place at the same time, it probably won't happen now. However, you can consider these people a **special class of acquaintances**.

Maintaining and cultivating even loose business relationships can create the environment for some serendipity to occur for you and those in your network. Some make the distinction that this is "farming," not "hunting."

Love your friends and family.

We consider friends and family to be in the same category because today the friends we choose are often as close, or closer, than blood relatives. Yet, as a society, we are losing touch with those closest to us.

Duke University and University of Arizona sociologists conducted a survey that revealed about **25 percent of those surveyed said they had no close friends at all**.

Most of those surveyed reported to have **only two confidants**, a drop of about a third from 1985-2004. The sociologists considered this drop "dramatic" (*American Sociological Review*, June 2006).

Duke's Lynn Smith-Lovin, Ph.D., commented, "This indicates something that's not good for our society. Ties with a close network of people create a safety net."

If you look at your own life, you may find that your business has cut into your social and family time. Friends may go weeks or months without talking to each other or enjoying a social event together.

We all can cite examples where we "just picked up where we left off," but that's not quite the same as continuing to build a friendship.

This is an issue for both men and women. E-mail or texting can keep the ties with friends and family from breaking, but the relationships may suffer from the lack of real communication.

The American Psychological Association warned of this issue more than a decade ago in the article "Isolation increases with Internet use." (www.apa.org September 1998).

"The technology that has allowed people to keep in closer touch with distant relatives and friends. . . is also replacing vital day-to-day human interactions. . . greater use of the Internet leads to shrinking social support and happiness."

Psychologist Robert Kraut, Ph.D., of Carnegie Mellon University, concluded, "We were surprised to find that what is a social technology, unlike television, has kind of antisocial consequences."

Over 10 years later, the situation hasn't improved.

The typical family has a crowded schedule and little time together. Couples connected by BlackBerrys and cell phones may have multiple interchanges daily, but find those messages are related to logistics: "Who's picking up Annie at ballet class?" "Can you pick up some milk on the way home?" "We're due at the Johnson's for dinner at 6:30. Don't forget."

Do you know anyone who thinks they connect often enough in a meaningful way with friends and family?

Cultivate acquaintances.

You meet someone on a plane. He's smart and interesting, but in an industry totally unrelated to yours. You exchange cards. The typical scenario is that you say nice things, pocket the card, and never see or hear from each other again. Ever.

What if. . . you sent a quick note after your trip to acknowledge that the conversation made the flight more enjoyable (or bearable, if the flight was anything but fun)? Just to be polite.

What if you also made a brief note, when you put his contact information into whatever database you use, about his love of golf and Cuban cigars?

A couple of months later, you clip a magazine article about organic tobacco production using time-honored hand-tilling and drop it in the mail with a Post-it® Note. Six months after that, you send a review of a new high-tech golf club.

What's the pay-off, you ask? Will this make him want to send work to me? Will I get a referral? Will we become friends? Do I have time for another friend? These are all valid questions, but you can't predict who is going to blossom from an acquaintance to a friend, colleague or referral source.

In the meantime, worst-case scenario, you're spreading good will, which is never a poor investment of time and effort.

And yet, there could be a business benefit as well, just not in a classic "X-marketing resulted in Y-business" kind of way. This is not marketing, but real relationship building. If you cultivate a large group of people normally on the fringes of your life, you can enrich both yourself and others.

You can become what Malcolm Gladwell (*Tipping Point,* 2002) calls "connectors," people who enjoy building acquaintanceships. He interviewed a **world-class connector**, Roger Horchow. Here's what Gladwell reported from that interview:

"I kept asking Horchow how all of the connections in his life had helped him in the business world, because I thought that the two things had to be linked, but the question seemed to puzzle him.

"It wasn't that his connections hadn't helped him. It was that he didn't think of his people collection as a business strategy. . . He simply likes people, in a genuine and powerful way, and he finds the patterns of acquaintanceship to be endlessly fascinating."

While not all of us have Roger Horchow's natural inclination to cultivate acquaintances, we can learn to open ourselves to letting new people into our lives.

Understand from the start that relationships don't have to be either close friends or nothing. . . a business relationship or nothing.

Gladwell explains **the importance of "weak ties,"** a concept out of Mark Granovetter's study, *Getting a Job.* The results of the study showed that when looking for a job, weak ties are better for referrals because. . .

". . . acquaintances, by definition, occupy a very different world than you. . . **Acquaintances, in short, represent a source of social power**, and the more acquaintances you have, the more powerful you are."

When you deliberately include acquaintances in your network that you contact periodically, you foster a certain warmth and connection.

The atmosphere you create with people invites the natural give and take of information, referrals and just plain good will. But your contacts with acquaintances must be free of selfish intent or hidden agenda. Otherwise you'll be labeled – and avoided – as a manipulator.

The Power of Relationships

Building relationships can have a more powerful and longer-lasting impact on **you personally**, the people in **your five circles**, and your **business** than anything you've ever done.

It doesn't replace normal marketing or advertising, but provides the **emotional connections** that bring people together.

Every satisfying and long-lasting relationship has these ten major characteristics. . .

1. Respect
2. Honesty
3. Attention
4. Warmth
5. Interest
6. Mutual give and take
7. Thoughtfulness
8. Humor
9. Support
10. Openness

This means, for example, you make sure your customers enjoy a sense of fairness in all your dealings. Your friends and family feel they're important, even with your busy schedule. Acquaintances feel good about knowing you.

You may wonder, "Is this hard to do? Is there a whole new skill set I need?" Not at all.

Here's the secret. . .

You learned everything you need to know from your Mom. Good relationships are based on **good manners**, plain and simple.

The list that follows shows the nine most common types of communications we have with people. Most of these apply whether you're talking with clients or business colleagues, family members or perfect strangers. The messages may be worded differently, depending on who's receiving them, but the sentiments are applicable to everyone.

These are the everyday courtesies that are the mark of a gracious person. But more importantly, they also are the communications that touch people personally and convey warmth and attention.

In a cell phone, e-mail, text message kind of world, these social graces become even more important. Technology has brought its own noise as well as isolation, so a message that says, "I was thinking especially about you" has a big impact.

Imagine what could happen in your business (and your life) if you cultivated acquaintances, prospects and customers – not just friends and family – as humans worth attention and respect?

"Hello!"

"Thank you."

"I have a surprise for you!"

"I'm sorry."

"I appreciate you."

"Thought you'd be interested in this."

"Congratulations!"

"Happy Birthday!"

"Have a special day!"

But how do you find the time?

The missing link – a Perpetual Contact System™.

You've likely heard the common phrase "people do business with people they know, like and trust." Bob Burg, author of *Winning Without Intimidation,* is one of numerous business authors who make this point.

While that's true, there's one more important element which marketing expert David Frey points out, "People will refer and do business with **people they remember**, like and trust."

When you follow our simple Perpetual Contact System, you'll develop a real relationship, which builds the "like and trust" part. And by being in contact on a regular basis, you'll be remembered. There won't be that moment when the person wonders, "Who is this from? Do I know him/her?"

That means when someone asks for a referral from a colleague in your network, it'll be **your name that's top-of-mind** and on the **tip of their tongue**.

In the next chapters, we elaborate on the importance of each one of these nine common communications. Then you'll find some simple plans that incorporate these very natural ways of interacting with people.

Summary. . .

▸ Open yourself to the idea that both close *and* casual relationships can enhance your life, as well as business.

▸ Become more aware of what's important to others so you can connect more meaningfully.

▸ Use everyday social interactions to make your contacts with people in your circles a natural expression of your interest in them.

CHAPTER 4

"Hello!"

Don't wait for people to be friendly. Show them how.
Anonymous

In this Chapter. . .

▸ "Hello" can be a passing greeting or the first step in building a relationship.

▸ Why your sense of overload causes you to make instant judgments on who to cultivate and who to ignore.

▸ How to say "Hello" to business and personal contacts – a list of messages to get you started.

Dale is a consultant to an upscale sporting goods manufacturer. He was going to New York for a trade show where his clients were exhibiting their new mountain bikes.

He knew he was going to take his clients to dinner one night, but he had only been to New York a couple of times and didn't know where he should take them. One of the clients traveled to New York frequently, so Dale wanted a place that was somewhat more interesting than the typical business restaurant.

He remembered he'd met a guy at a golf tournament – Joe. . . John . . . maybe Jerry. After digging in his desk, he finally found the card: Jeff Landon. He called the number and reached Jeff's voice mail.

Dale left a message. "Uh, oh, hi Jeff. Dale Gardner here. We met at the golf tournament in Phoenix last August. You may not remember me. Gordy Jensen introduced us.

"Well, anyway, I remember you said you spent a lot of time in New York on business. I'm heading there myself and I'm hoping you can give me a recommendation for a restaurant that's not too trendy, but is popular with the locals. . ."

Jeff, unfortunately, only vaguely recalled meeting Dale. By the time he returned the call, Dale was already in New York.

In a minute I'll show you what Dale could have done differently when he met Jeff, if he'd had a Perpetual Contact System in place. What a different outcome!

◆ ◆ ◆

The opportunities of "Hello."

We say "Hello" throughout the day to people we know and total strangers including friends, associates and grocery store cashiers.

In this chapter, "Hello" signals the moment when you meet a total stranger, perhaps someone at a conference, on a plane or through someone you know.

"Hello" is filled with possibilities. You never know when even a chance meeting will turn into something significant. The mistake we make is to brush by first "Hellos" without much thought.

Of course, the opposite can also be true. Aggressive marketers can turn "Hello" into nothing short of an assault if their intention at, say, a convention is to gather leads without even knowing if you have interest in what they're selling.

These are also the misled folks who either decide you *will* buy from them, or conversely, they turn on their heel when they find out you're of no use to them.

Yet, don't we all do some sort of filtering like this, even if we're a bit more subtle?

Snap judgments limit opportunities.

Here are the ways we typically filter people when meeting them (excluding "filters" we use when looking for a date or mate). . .

> ▶ Nice and interesting, but I have so many people I don't keep up with already. Pass.

▶ Nice guy. Obviously not a prospect. Next.

▶ Possible prospect. Get contact information.

▶ Well connected. Might be a referral source. Get cozy as fast as possible.

▶ Obvious prospect. Pounce.

Okay. What's going on here? **The filter is usually all about us**, what we're looking for and what would benefit ourselves.

What if... you turned the tables and in a completely non-possessive, no-agenda way, listened for and responded to a need or interest in the other person?

Here's what Dale could have done. . .

When Dale met Jeff in Phoenix, he took the time to find out where Jeff lived, where he traveled and other details that wouldn't be considered too personal for acquaintances to share as small talk. They both spent a lot of time on the road and even discovered they stayed in the same hotels in certain cities.

Since both loved to golf, they decided to stay in touch so if they ever wound up in the same city at the same time, they could play 18 holes at a local course together.

As soon as he returned home after the weekend tournament, Dale sent Jeff a note, including his home phone number, and jotted down the cities he was scheduled to visit in the next three months. Jeff responded by e-mailing his schedule to Dale.

Dale would note where Jeff was going to be and send a restaurant recommendation or a clipping from the local paper about a sporting event coming up. Jeff started doing the same.

So when Dale called, Jeff greeted him like an old friend. "Hey buddy. What's up? Are we going to be in Columbus at the same time in May?"

"Not sure yet, but I'll let you know. I was calling to get a quick tip about where to take a client in New York, Upper East Side. Somewhere locals like, but not one of the usual business restaurants."

"Oh sure. There's a great sushi place near Lexington and 56th. I eat there all the time when I'm in New York. Owner's name is Ray. I'll e-mail you the info so you can make a reservation. Tell him you want the table where I always sit. It's out of the traffic pattern and quieter. If you need to talk business, it's the best table in the place."

Dale and Jeff corresponded every few months and even golfed together a few times when they were in the same city. As they found more common ground and developed a level of trust, they started making referrals to each other throughout the year.

Did they become best friends? No. But they did develop a cordial relationship that went far beyond the usual social and business relationship of mere acquaintances.

It's easy to see **the difference real contact makes**.

Note these important differences between what Dale did to build a relationship in the second scenario and what most business people would do:

> ▸ He **had no pre-determined agenda** in staying in touch with Jeff except to build a connection – a casual relationship – built on their mutual interests.

> ▸ Jeff helped Dale out, not because he had to, or felt obligated, but **because he wanted to**. They made referrals out of mutual interest in each other's success.

> ▸ They **weren't business associates or even close friends** in the classic sense, and yet they both were enriched in small ways that make a difference. . . and take **little time or effort** on either side.

The first step is to get contact information and a little more.

In the '80s, I was introduced to a lawyer whose entire credenza was covered with neat boxes filled with 3 x 5 file cards. I was fascinated and asked about them – as, apparently, many others had before me.

He said he had made it a goal to capture contact information on every person he met in the course of business, social/business events and political functions from the time he was in law school.

Even with this cumbersome, manual system (this was in the early '80s), he was able to keep track of the top people on the list, where they were, and their expertise and connections.

Dozens, maybe hundreds, of these contacts didn't result in any meaningful connections, but his top group – far larger and better cultivated than most – would take his calls and do their best to provide phone numbers, valuable resources and information. He would do the same for them.

Why did he collect information on that many people? We can assume he was like a kid on the beach picking up one pebble after another because he didn't know which ones would be valuable to him until later.

But even the seldom-accessed cards put him within one or two degrees of top political and corporate leaders in his own state, as well as the highest officials in Washington, D.C.

Although none of us can welcome every acquaintance we meet into our lives, there's also no reason to disregard all acquaintances, especially those who share interests, industries and common ground.

If the life-enhancing aspects of keeping in touch lightly don't interest you, recall our previous reference about acquaintances being the best referrers for a job, from Malcolm Gladwell's *Tipping Point*, which stated that a major study found,

". . . 55.6 percent saw their contact only 'occasionally.' Twenty-eight percent saw the contact 'rarely.'

"People weren't getting their jobs through their friends. They were getting them through their acquaintances."

What about business referrals?

Do statistics for acquaintance referrals hold true for business referrals? We have no similar studies to tell us. However, as stated before, people do tend to **refer who they know, like, trust. . . and remember**.

Jennie Bond, formerly the BBC's royal correspondent, said, "The Duke of Edinburgh has perfected the art of saying hello and goodbye in the same handshake."

That might work for the royals, but the rest of us could be surprised at the positive outcomes of being more open to those we meet.

Think of the times you met someone who seemed interesting. You wanted to stay in touch but never got around to making even the first contact.

So it wasn't your lack of interest, or maybe even the time. Could it be you simply **didn't know what kind of contact would be appropriate**? Or you didn't know what to say? Were you unsure whether the person even wanted to hear from you?

Here are some examples of "common ground". . .

When you first meet someone, in the course of conversation, you might find out any number of things about their interests and passions, hobbies, etc. You may share their interests, or know of people or resources that would be useful to them.

One or more of these could be the springboard to making a connection with almost any individual. . .

- Hobbies – art, music, fishing, gardening, etc.
- Sports – teams they like and sports they play
- Books – favorite authors, titles and topics
- Movies – types of movies they enjoy, most recently watched DVDs, favorite actors
- Travel – favorite locations for vacations, best accommodations, most exciting attractions, most beautiful locations, or friendliest people

▸ Food – preferred ethnic foods, most memorable meals, favorite restaurants, foods they like to cook at home, big parties or small get-togethers

All of the topics are considered "safe." At this stage of acquaintanceship, you want to avoid dicey topics like religion, politics and medical problems.

Notice that these are the kinds of light "small talk" topics that people discuss at parties. Most people like to think they're above small talk, but truly it's the verbal grease in many social wheels.

If you listen, you'll be able to mine the conversation for ideas about what to say in a follow-up that will "connect" with them.

Get permission to follow up.

In the online world, marketers must have permission to send an e-mail to another person. This is usually obtained when someone opts in to your mailing list or requests information.

If you use a service such as AWeber, the system automatically sends a confirmation e-mail that prompts the recipient to validate their request. This double opt-in is the gold standard for permission marketing online.

Even in social situations, it's wise to say something like, "You know, I came across an article about [their favorite thing] recently. Would you like me to send it to you?"

Or, if it's apparent from a brief conversation that you have mutual friends, interests or other connections you both want to follow up on later, it's certainly all right to say, "It seems we have a lot of common interests. Would you mind if I contacted you some time?"

Some people are so overloaded, or protective of their privacy, they will decline. Let it go. But if they say yes, get their preferred e-mail address or mailing address.

Terrie Williams suggests in *The Personal Touch* "...don't flat-out say to someone, 'Can I have your card?' Instead ask: 'Is there a way I can get in touch with you?'"

**Here are some ways to say "Hello"
or follow up on a face-to-face "Hello"...**

1. **Send a simple "Nice to meet you" follow-up**. This will be most memorable if sent by mail. However, the faster you contact your new acquaintance the better. If you know you'll be slow getting out a note, use e-mail, providing the recipient said it's all right.

   This can be a way to also provide the contact information that isn't on your business card. For example, you can list the social/business networks you're on, such as Linked-In, Plaxo, etc. If you have an alternate e-mail address or phone number, you may want to give it to them, as well.

   Offering additional contact information, especially to business contacts, conveys the welcoming message, "Other people can contact me through normal channels, but you can reach me through my private number and personal e-mail."

2. **Share a photo**. This is one of the easiest and most natural things to send. At an event, snap digital photos with a pocket camera or cell phone – either of you and the individual, a group, or some picture-worthy moment that will be amusing or memorable.

3. **Share a news link**. It's likely that you'll meet many individuals at certain meetings, conferences and conventions who share common interests. Sign up on Web sites and reputable blogs to pick up news and information of interest to these people.

   Send the link to the item via e-mail with a quick note that you thought it would be of interest.

4. **Share a YouTube link**. Once you know someone's interest, you can find humorous, instructive or inspirational videos at YouTube with a few keywords. You can e-mail through a link on the video's page, or copy/paste into your own e-mail program.

▸ **Mail a tear sheet.** Rip an article out of a magazine or newspaper and attach a Post-it® Note or your business card. A simple "Did you see this?" message is sufficient. Even if they did see it, your thoughtfulness will make an impact.

By making the effort to follow up, you will be in a tiny minority of people who actively cultivate acquaintances. The follow-up alone will go a long way to locking your name into the memory of the recipient, which will prevent the "Who is this?" when you contact them next time.

Your periodic contacts will keep you on the radar of your acquaintances. As you progress through the nine most common communications, you'll see how they can be adapted to maintain and sustain a friendly, though casual, contact.

Summary. . .

▸ If you "connect" with a person on some level at the "Hello" face-to-face event, it's worth adding them to your network of acquaintances.

▸ "Confirm" your introduction or meeting with a light communication that carries no obligation, including the obligation to respond.

▸ As you review the remaining eight common, everyday interactions, you'll see that you don't need special skills to make contact with a light, but warm touch.

Sending a card to someone you just met
will not only make you memorable for your thoughtfulness,
but serve as the first step in building a cordial relationship.

Hi Jeff,

It was great to meet you at the conference last week
in New York. Hope the weather didn't interfere with your
trip home.

You and I seem to share quite a few interests and goals. If
I can ever provide any support to you, feel free to call my
private number, 555-555-1234.

Warmest regards,

Scott Murphy
scott@spmurphyconsulting.com

CHAPTER 5

"Thank you."

The deepest craving of human nature
is the need to be appreciated.
William James

In this Chapter. . .

▸ Why, if you do nothing else, you should send thank-you notes.

▸ Proof that thank-you notes are the mark of business leaders.

▸ When to write a thank-you note.

▸ How to write a thank-you note.

Sherry was a sweet, shy and very talented makeup artist. She had refined her art while working on actors for films, guests for TV shows, and models for fashion shows.

Even though Sherry was talented and respected, she knew there were assignments she was missing because her name wasn't "top-of-mind" among those who could hire her. Without any marketing experience, and truthfully, a fairly small circle of business associates to market to, she didn't know what was appropriate or would make a difference.

She turned to us for marketing advice. We gave her a simple plan that required nothing but sending thank-you notes to people she worked with.

The plan was affordable and easy to implement. We encouraged her to get a supply of cards and stamps. At the end of the day, she'd go home, write notes to the people who had hired her for the day's assignment, stamp the envelope and mail the note.

To make sure she didn't carry the note around for days before mailing it, she simply put it in her mailbox at the end of the driveway for pick up.

We also encouraged her to send thank-you notes to her co-workers for referrals and to other colleagues who made any effort to help her in her career.

She appreciated that the "thank-you plan" was so simple, required very little time, and was completely without the aggressive and manipulative techniques used by others in the business.

Her simple gratitude was a natural extension of her personality and made her stand out as a class act and, in fact, did keep her top-of-mind when assignments were booked.

• • •

Saying "thank you" is important for smooth social and business relationships. It's not old-fashioned and it never went out of style, even though the practice has fallen into widespread disuse.

When your business is built on personal relationships, "thank you" is not an option. Sending a "thank you" says something about you. Not sending a "thank you" says something else.

For small business owners and independent professionals, thank-you notes can provide an enormous advantage. As mentioned earlier, larger companies can make contact, but rarely can they make a real, personal connection with individuals.

If you do nothing else, send thank-you notes because. . .

Successful professionals always say, "Thank you."

Robert Half International, a financial recruiting agency, uncovered surprising information in a survey.

The survey revealed that "76 percent of business executives take into account post-interview thank-you notes when evaluating job candidates. Unfortunately, only 36 percent of candidates send them."

As an independent business person, you may not be interviewing for a job. . . or are you? Consultants, freelancers and other service providers are often interviewed before an assignment is given.

Even those in the trades compete for work, whether it's for a kitchen remodel or new landscaping.

Without a follow-up "thank you" for the opportunity to be considered, you lose the chance to let the prospect know you want the business. That's a needless waste of a good lead.

Here's what leading business people and publications say. . .

▸ Donald Trump believes that thank-you notes can have a positive impact on business. In her book, *Business Class* (2005), author Jacqueline Whitmore quoted Trump.

"Not only will people remember that you took the time to write," The Donald told her, "they will also consider you thoughtful, responsible, and aware. These are good attributes to have in business."

▸ Stanley Marcus, the driving force of Neiman Marcus from 1950-1975, said, "Look at art. Laugh. Collect something. Do your job well. Look closely at all the details in life. Be aware and be curious. Write thank-you notes."

▸ Jack Mitchell is CEO of the successful Mitchell/Richards/Marsh's clothing stores. In his book, *Hug Your Customers*, he says, "One of the best hugs of all is a letter of thanks. . . The first-time customer is extremely important because first impressions are so powerful."

Mitchell himself picked up the idea from the tour company, Tauck World Discovery, which sent personal, hand-signed letters to travelers following each tour. He sends hundreds of thank-you notes every year.

▸ Sam Glenn is CEO of Everything Attitude and author of *A Kick in the Attitude* (2007). Kathryn Tuggle quoted Glenn in "BlackBerrys Be Damned: Can You Do Business Without Them?" (www.foxbusiness.com, June 28, 2008).

"Tech can't make up for the experience you create when you have a personal meeting with somebody. In my first job out of college, my boss made us find two people on a weekly basis to write thank-you notes to.

"I've been doing that for 15 years now, and there is always somebody to thank. It's personal and meaningful because it's not electronic."

> In the article "Ten Ways to Thank Your Clients with Pizazz" (*LAN* June 1995), Roger Fuller concluded, ". . . continuously thanking customers for their business is one of the most vital parts of my job. I'm sure that for true professionals, this is always the case."

> Joanna L. Krotz, in the article "The Power of Saying Thank You" at the Microsoft Small Business Center (www.microsoft.com), states, "Today, extending old-time courtesies helps you stand out. . . saying 'thank you' has become a competitive advantage. . . remembering to do so is a sales point of difference.

"It also goes a long way toward forging the relationships that can turn into opportunities."

> A survey by Lenox, the gift company, revealed that only 50 percent of U.S. adults surveyed said they always send a thank-you note after they receive a gift. Denise Dinyon, the Lenox etiquette maven, said, "It appears that the fast-paced, high-tech existence may have taken a toll on the civility in today's society."

You can see that the need for a simple "thank you" is a basic human desire, regardless of the setting or situation.

Thanks may be ignored by many, but as a small business owner or independent professional, gratitude that prompts a sincere "thank you" can create a warm connection like nothing else.

If you think a thank-you note is too much bother, recall the wisdom of G. B. Stern, 20th-century British novelist, playwright and biographer: "Silent gratitude isn't much use to anyone."

When to write a thank-you note.

In social situations, any time you have received a gift, been a guest for a meal, been hosted for one or more nights at someone's home. . . or any time someone did you a favor or said something on your behalf, a "thank you" should be sent.

Here's a list of common instances when thanks are called for. . .

1. a lead
2. lunch
3. a helpful or friendly call
4. any help provided
5. information you requested
6. useful, unsolicited information
7. kind words; compliments
8. a reference
9. a referral
10. any kind of support

Mailed "thank you" notes are still the strongest option.

Sure, you can send a quick e-mail to say thanks. You can send an e-mail greeting card from any number of sites today.

But nothing has the impact of a personal "thank you" that arrives in the mail. Nothing.

Many years ago, Crane Fine Stationery placed full-page ads in magazines. A woman was hugging a letter close to her. The headline read, "To the best of our knowledge, no one ever cherished a fax."

Later in the book, I'll tell you about the service we recommend – Send Out Cards – that lets you create a thank-you note online in your own handwriting. The service prints, stamps and mails it for you.

The two cardinal rules are. . .
Make them SHORT and send them FAST.

A diplomat once said, "The sooner you say thank you, the less you have to say."

Think about it. How many times have you received or sent a thank you that started and ended with an apology for being so long overdue?

The reason saying "thank you" is so hard for most people isn't because they aren't grateful, but they simply don't know what to say.

There are many ways to craft a thank-you note, but we prefer a simple and highly effective 3-point approach. This structure means you can express sincere, even heartfelt, thanks in as few as three sentences. (You can say more if you like, of course.)

For illustration, there are three business situations where a thank you is needed: an important call, lunch, and flowers to mark a promotion. These are easier than you think.

Part 1: The opening is the thank you.

Thanks so much for the call.

Thanks for lunch!

The beautiful floral arrangement arrived today and it's incredible. Thank you!

Part 2: Elaborate with a personal comment relating to the gesture you're thanking the person for.

It was great to get the news about [fill in the blank].

It was a welcome sanity break. You make me laugh so hard!

It was a wonderful surprise. You're so very thoughtful.

Part 3: Wrap it up quickly. Use this to solidify the relationship. Add a thoughtful comment or suggest the next time to get together.

I appreciate your taking time out of your busy schedule to touch base.

Let's choose a day to get together again [suggested time]. My treat.

Thanks so much for celebrating with me.

Your final note will flow like these. . .

Thanks so much for the call. It was great to get the news about Bill's promotion. I appreciate your taking time out of your busy schedule to touch base.

Thanks for lunch! It was a welcome sanity break. You make me laugh so hard! Let's choose a day to get together again after I get back from Phoenix. My treat.

The beautiful floral arrangement arrived today and it's incredible. Thank you! It was a wonderful surprise. You're so very thoughtful. Thanks for celebrating with me.

Add your usual sign-off, such as *Best regards* or *Sincerely yours*, and you're done.

By following the above construction, you can get a note written in a matter of minutes.

Summary. . .

▸ Writing thank-you notes will mark you as a thoughtful professional with class.

▸ Send your thanks as quickly as possible.

▸ It's not difficult to write a note if you follow the three-point structure.

*A thank-you note never goes unnoticed,
because receiving one is becoming increasingly rare.*

I can no other answer make, but, thanks, and thanks.
William Shakespeare

Dear Bob,

Thank you for the referral to Jim Winston at the Candoro Group. We have a preliminary meeting scheduled May 14.

Your strong recommendation was key to securing the appointment so easily. I deeply appreciate the referral and will let you know the outcome of the meeting.

Best regards,

Larry

CHAPTER 6

"I appreciate you."

There is more hunger for love and appreciation in this world than for bread.

Mother Teresa

In this Chapter. . .

▸ Why appreciation is essential to relationships.

▸ How to convey your appreciation to customers and clients.

▸ Who deserves recognition and why.

Jerry and Sarah started their accounting business together after both had spent several years at a large accounting firm. They had a vision of bringing the same quality of advice and service to small businesses that was available to large companies. Both were efficient, sharp professionals who knew the tax laws inside out.

There was no question their credentials were sterling, so it hadn't been difficult to attract clients. The company grew and soon they had a staff of six helping with various facets of the business.

However, after just three years, they started to lose a few key clients and staff turnover was alarmingly high. The two partners were completely baffled. Their work was professional and prompt. They had shown their clients how to save significantly on taxes. Employees were paid well.

A colleague happened to be friendly with executives at two of the defecting clients. Jerry asked him to discreetly inquire why the clients had left. Both were stunned by the feedback he'd been able to get from the clients.

"It wasn't your work," their friend told them. "Neither client found fault with your work. But both reported they simply didn't feel like you valued them as clients and that it wouldn't make any difference to you if they stayed or left.

"You did the work with precision, but never showed any real appreciation. Your attention to winning their business vanished almost as soon as you landed their accounts."

This revelation made them wonder if the same was true of the staff. Sarah asked her personal assistant if the reasons employees gave for leaving were the real reasons, or just excuses.

She hesitated and finally admitted, "Yes, you pay well, but you also ask us to do a lot of extra work as if it's expected. Sam, Julie and Ben all left because they felt their contributions were invisible to you."

Finally, both Jerry and Sarah realized that proficiency alone wasn't enough to bond them to clients or employees.

• • •

In the previous chapter we discussed thank-you notes, which are most often sent in response to a gift or favor. Appreciation and gratitude may also trigger a thank-you note; however, it can be expressed in many other small or spectacular ways.

In this chapter, the focus is on appreciation for your primary business relationships: customers or clients, employees and vendors.

There are many ways to show gratitude to friends, family and business buddies as well. However, showing appreciation to those directly involved in your business is critical to long-term success.

People are people in social situations and business. Yet in business, we often persist in ignoring basic human needs and shift into the more impersonal, transactional mode that diminishes the human touch.

Jerry and Sarah had every reason to think that once a client was secured, their worries were over. Their professional skills were top level. Small business clients were grateful for their expertise. Yet they lost accounts because they relied almost exclusively on their proficiency, never considering the importance of appreciation in maintaining the clients.

It was invisible to them that Mother Teresa's wisdom applies across the board: people need love and appreciation.

In America, we spend so much time working, it's more important than ever to generate humanity in the marketplace. Adopting a grateful attitude has a positive impact on you, your customers or clients, and your employees and vendors.

If you think this is intuitive to all authors of leading business books targeting the corporate market, it is not. In the lengthy, well-researched, corporation-oriented books on customer retention and loyalty in our personal library, there's little or no mention of customer appreciation as part of an effective strategy.

Again, this is why you, as a small business owner, a professional in private practice, or a service provider, have an advantage by building real relationships through courtesy, attention and respect.

Customers and clients are attracted to those who show appreciation.

Showing appreciation is an everyday thing and, except for special events, it's free or costs very little. In fact, when you ask why someone is especially enthusiastic about a particular company, it often tracks to one of two things, or a combination of both. . .

1. The customer or client enjoys consistently good service and cordial attention.

2. A single memorable action on the part of someone at the company made a lasting impression.

In *Hug Your Customer,* Jack Mitchell says, "Everything revolves around the customer. Everyone says the customer is important, but in most businesses, actions speak otherwise. . .

"In the simplest sense, a hug is anything that exceeds a customer's expectations."

In one of the many extra-mile stories Mitchell retells, he literally gave a customer "the coat off his back." The customer was flying out of town and needed a navy blue cashmere top coat immediately.

His stores were out of stock and the gray coat Mitchell offered wasn't what the customer wanted. For the trip, Mitchell lent the customer his own navy cashmere coat, which he had worn to the man's office.

And while a well-timed, spontaneous gesture is memorable, treating people well on a consistent basis also makes a big impact. We've all endured sales clerks who ignore customers while they huddle for a private conversation.

Many people deal almost exclusively with customers and clients by phone. With that being the main point of contact, it's always surprising to find yourself treated as an interruption to their day.

This story puts that upside-down service attitude in perspective. A friend and his son went into a well-known sandwich chain. No one was in sight behind the counter. They called "Hello?" to see if the staff was in the back.

A disgruntled young woman came out of the back kitchen area where she had been working. She was in a foul mood and prepared their order with a side of contempt. Another family came in the door and she kicked into a higher gear of disgust. She complained, "With all these people interrupting me, how am I supposed to get my work done?"

What we can see as obvious in others, we miss in ourselves. We probably all know shop owners who busy themselves in the back office and rarely talk to customers or supervise the clerks who do.

You may also know, as we do, consultants and service providers who deal with clients at their own convenience, conveying that they are more important than those they serve.

Of course, if you work alone or have a small staff, you do have some juggling to do. But those we serve should never feel like an inconvenience, when making them feel special is so simple.

Insightful Business Ideas is a blog published by Tom Titlow, a small business consultant. In one post, "Customer Appreciation and Gratitude, Why Saying

Thank You is So Important" (www.greatbusinessideas. com, September 18, 2007), he made these important observations. . .

Appreciation is ". . . part of who you are as a person and as a business owner. It is not something that you do when times are tough and business is slow."

It won't be effective ". . . if you aren't truly grateful for every single one of your customers."

Two different studies found different statistics, but identified the same underlying problem for businesses that don't convey a caring attitude toward customers and clients. . .

1. A survey from The Rockefeller Corporation was cited in *U.S. News & World Report,* which noted the number one reason customers leave is the perception of indifference. In other words, they felt the business – or someone representing the company – just didn't care.

2. A second study is reported in a white paper, "The Loyalty Connection: Secrets to Customer Retention," produced by Right Now Technologies (www.rightnow.com). The respondents overwhelmingly reported – 73 percent – that customer service was the reason they left.

   Further, the study showed that the business owners or managers themselves believed only 21 percent of the people who left did so due to customer service, blaming price as the number one cause of customer defections.

This last piece of information lets us know that companies can engage in disastrous self-deception about how customers and clients view them.

It's a legitimate concern to ask, "What can a small – even micro – business like mine do to keep clients and customers happy?"

Candidly, good manners will often be your best asset. Kindness, respect, warmth and a willingness to go the extra mile are in short supply in the high-speed, get-ahead culture.

However, you can also. . .

- ▶ Send a personal note. Even when you don't have a specific reason to send a thank-you note, an expression of gratitude is always appropriate and welcome.

- ▶ Use some of the ideas in the next chapter, "I have a surprise for you," to express your appreciation.

- ▶ Send cards or personal notes (and flowers or gifts when appropriate) for special birthdays, a child's achievements, weddings, anniversaries, during an illness or in sympathy.

- ▶ Give your clients or customers first pick of sale products, seminar seats, copies of your new book, etc., so they know you value them and give them preference.

- ▶ Hold special customer appreciation events. Throw a party at your place of business or a favorite restaurant.

- ▶ Employ what you have at hand to make the right impression. An upscale cosmetic dentist in Dallas is located in a high-rise office building that features a popular café on the ground floor.

  The spouse or friend, who will drive the groggy patient home, can relax in the restaurant with coffee and a pastry (or even breakfast or lunch) instead of waiting in the dentist's lobby. "Just tell them to put it on my tab" is a most surprising gesture of hospitality.

When you fully adopt the "appreciation mindset," you'll be more alert as you observe and listen to your customers. Their comments will tip you off to the things that would be meaningful to them.

Employees need appreciation, too.

This is a shocking statistic, but *The Carrot Principle* (2007) by Adrian Gostick and Chester Elton, noted that **79 percent** – almost eight out of every 10 – employees who quit their jobs said they **left because they didn't feel appreciated**.

In the classic movie, *North Dallas Forty,* Nick Nolte says to the team owners, "We're not the team. . . We're the equipment."

At some level, employees who feel like they're only "the equipment" want to find more meaning – and recognition – for their contributions.

If you're withholding honest praise or gratitude, you may unwittingly be sowing seeds of discontent that could cost you a valuable employee. That's a problem you can easily avoid.

On his blog, Tom Titlow encouraged business owners to open up and let employees know that what they do has real value (www.greatbusinessideas.com blog post, September 8, 2007).

"Take time out to show them how they make a difference as an individual. . . When you show them how they make a difference, they will want to make more of a difference."

How do you show gratitude?

▸ Say so. A quick in-the-hall, "Hey Rob, those were great points you made in the meeting" can make someone's day. Acknowledgment is gratifying. One caution: it must be sincere.

▸ Spread the credit. A few co-workers who've knocked themselves out to get your presentation ready will appreciate it when you credit them with helping land a new account. Ignore their contribution, or claim the credit yourself, at your own risk.

▸ Compliment someone's efforts "behind their back." People are used to only hearing criticism leak back to them from confidential conversations. Praise will get back to them as well.

▸ Celebrate when the team completes a major project, especially if it involved extra hours or ingenuity to complete. Ad agencies frequently have high-stakes deadlines. Often, when complete, the company pays for an afternoon off for a picnic and Frisbee tournament or some other low-tech, high-level fun.

▸ Offer some flexibility. Flex time has been around for a while, but people still needed to be in the office. A more recent option is Best Buy's ROWE – Results-Only-Work-Environment. People can work when and how they like as long as they produce the work.

Although tech companies, among others, have enjoyed similar flexibility, Best Buy committed to shape the cultural code around their ROWE "experiment" and now teach others the process through CultureRX. The major development is the inclusion of all employees, not just a privileged few.

Granted, the nature of many small businesses may require personnel to be present at specific times. It's tough to wait on tables virtually, after all. However, it makes sense to allow office workers who are tied to their computers to work where and when they are happier and more productive.

In fact, Best Buy reported (NBC News, March 15, 2007) that productivity is up 35 percent. Turnover and low morale are almost non-existent. It may not technically be appreciation to offer such a solution, but it is respectful of hard-working employees.

▸ Think of the families. Host family nights at the movies. You don't have to go as a group, but you can supply the tickets and vouchers for snacks. Plan a picnic. Give a gift certificate for a romantic dinner for an employee and a spouse or partner for a job well done.

▸ Support favorite employee charities. There are many ways to do this, based on the size of your business and budget. Contributing to their charities financially is one option, but it might make more sense to host a fund-raising event.

▸ Allow everyone to share in the goodies when vendors send gifts.

These are only ideas to get you started. Just be sure to think "inclusive" not "exclusive" when you're passing out the praise.

If you have a star player who gets the spotlight all the time, this will backfire on you. Everyone is making a contribution or, we assume, they wouldn't be there. Show appreciation in a way that will build team effort, not sabotage it.

There are excellent books to help you, including *1001 Ways to Reward Employees* by Bob Nelson (2005).

Vendors are people, too.

We often forget our tolerant vendors, the ones who jump through hoops to make our businesses work, and make us look good in the process. We expect them to shower us with goodies for providing business to them. But it's also a great idea to shower them with appreciation for doing all they do, often under trying circumstances.

I personally learned the value of this early in my career as an account executive at an ad agency. There seemed to be a rule that printers scheduled important jobs only in the middle of the night. It wasn't at all unusual to be in the pressroom with a massive Heidelberg churning out proofs for my approval at 2:00 a.m.

Pressmen are proud of their skill. Having the client on the floor to approve a proof can be. . . challenging. I began making homemade cookies to take with me on the midnight runs. I rarely had a problem with the men, even if we, together, had some problems getting the colors right.

When my employer discovered that the secret to my success in getting cooperation was cookies, he was skeptical. He said, "They shouldn't need cookies to get it right. That's their job." However, I didn't stop.

After one particularly difficult job that went from the day shift to the night shift (with me on the night shift), the peanut butter cookies (the night shift's favorite) saved everyone's sanity while we got the color corrected.

In the morning, there was great surprise at the office that I'd been able to get it right, with the night crew, after all. I explained what we'd gone through to get it done. My employer asked, "Why can't the rest of us get that out of them?"

"You don't take them peanut butter cookies," I answered.

A silly solution of an inexperienced account executive? At that early stage of my career, I needed something to get the men to work with me and not stand in opposition to me just to demand respect for their expertise. The cookies somehow conveyed my respect and honest appreciation.

Plus, the night crew, of all people, rarely got any kind words or special treatment. I do believe I pulled better work out of the shop than many who had more technical expertise. I wasn't an outsider to those men. I was welcome. I was on their side.

How can you show appreciation to vendors? I've hired vendors and I've been one, so this is my biased list. . .

- ▶ If your vendor is a freelancer or independent consultant working some of the time on site, include them in the "team" celebrations mentioned for employees.

  The line is very blurry today between employees and contractors. Sometimes it's only a matter of how someone is paid that makes the distinction.

- ▶ Be specific. It's nice to give broad compliments like, "You guys always do good work." However it's more powerful to say, and often more appreciated, if you're specific. "Everyone at the office was amazed that you could turn that project in three days."

  Contractors are in the business of jumping through hoops. Please notice when they do.

- ▶ Throw a vendor appreciation party. If you're a small business owner, or especially an independent professional or contractor, you probably rely on a support network of people to help you do what you do. If that's the case, keep in mind that you're only as good as your suppliers.

Invite them to your office, home or a restaurant for a party. It doesn't need to be lavish, just fun.

▸ Recognize the individual players on your team. It's one thing to do something special for the head guy and a totally different thing to let the individuals who are behind the scenes bask in your praise.

If you're thinking of sending a big box of chocolates for the whole office, consider instead a basket with individual boxes and personal notes to all concerned. I can almost guarantee they will do back flips for you next time.

▸ Send individual notes of appreciation. It's rare enough that people thank vendors at all, so taking the time to write a personal note will have a big impact. (It has the added benefit of getting you "bonus points" with a vendor that can translate to more generous terms or extra effort when you really need it.)

Summary. . .

▸ Most people feel some level of appreciation deprivation and can use some attention.

▸ Show appreciation whenever and however you can. A verbal compliment is welcome; a written note is memorable.

▸ Be sincere. People know when they've done something worth acknowledging. They'll appreciate a single honest expression of gratitude over three thin ones.

▸ Everyone who helps you in business is worthy of your gratitude. Spread it liberally wherever it's deserved. It doesn't cost you anything.

Appreciation is one of the best gifts
you can give anyone.

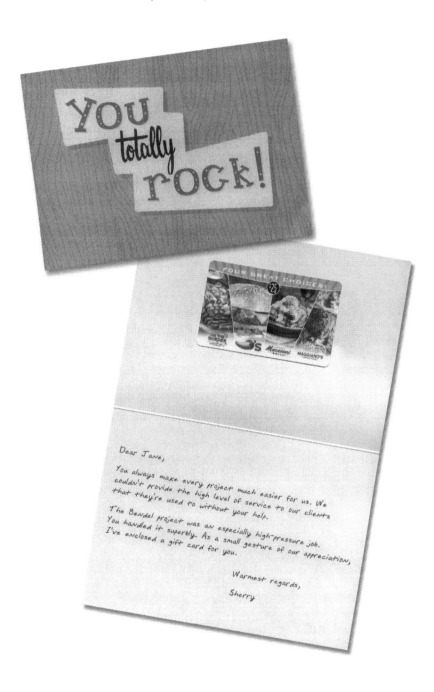

CHAPTER 7

"I have a surprise for you!"

Surprise is where creativity comes in.
Ray Bradbury

In this Chapter. . .

▶ How upbeat surprises strengthen your personal and business relationships.

▶ Why you benefit when you surprise others.

▶ The simple things you can do to surprise others.

Jake enjoyed surprising others. In college, his surprises weren't always welcome, as they came in the form of elaborate practical jokes that embarrassed his friends.

However, after a couple of pranks backfired, leaving good friends humiliated and angry, he realized that people like surprises, but only when they're fun or generate warmth, acceptance and thoughtfulness.

So when Jake became a sales rep for a major equipment firm after graduation, he began using his natural inclination to surprise people to build connections with prospects, customers and friends.

Often the surprise was something of little value, but of great significance to the recipient. Once, he'd been able to get an autograph of the starting quarterback of a client's favorite football team. Another time, he came across an out-of-print book a friend had mentioned she couldn't find.

These types of surprises required him to listen more carefully to people. Nevertheless, as his network of contacts expanded, there were many he didn't see on a regular basis. That didn't keep him from surprising them.

On one occasion, a business book was published of special interest to individuals in his field. Jake ordered a hundred books at a special volume price. He wrote a personal note to each of his top 100 customers and sent them with the books.

Another time, he had boxes of chocolate chip cookies sent to the secretary or assistant of ten key customers on Administrative Professionals Day.

Jake enjoys "making smiles" as he calls it. "I don't surprise people with the idea that I'll get anything back but good will."

That doesn't stop his customers from talking up Jake and his business. They have opened some very big doors for him.

• • •

Jake is on to something. Everyone has a busy life filled with many surprises that are not happy – from a bounced check to a mistake on an order, a rent increase to a child dropping out of college.

When you switch from a *transactional* mindset to a *relational* one, you begin to **see everyone in your personal network in more human terms**. You see ways to make their lives a little easier, more fun, or less stressed.

For some people, reaching out to others is natural. They simply can't help themselves when it comes to making life more fun, exciting and adventurous for others. If this isn't natural, you can learn the skill.

The principle has been applied liberally to business because it works. When shoppers are offered samples in Whole Foods, Costco, Sam's or your local grocery store, for example, they buy.

Robert B. Cialdini, Ph.D., is a recognized authority in persuasion, compliance and negotiation. The 5th edition of his book, *Influence: Science and Practice*, was released in August, 2008.

Cialdini's six "weapons of influence" are powerful – the weapons of choice for marketers. The first weapon is reciprocation – which, simply stated, is that people tend to return a favor, or may even feel obligated to do so.

How you apply the reciprocity principle will be a reflection of your values. We've seen some business people who are, by nature, generous and open-hearted, while others use the principle in a way that could only be described as manipulative.

We recommend adopting an attitude that's open-handed and open-hearted as opposed to self-serving.

But aside from how you apply reciprocation in a sales situation, when you're building relationships. . .

Thoughtful acts benefit you because in giving, you always receive.

In creating an environment that's filled with happy surprises, it's best if you **don't worry where the payback comes from**. The overall idea behind developing your five relationship circles is to have a network (and access to other networks) that creates important connections for yourself and others.

Apart from the benefits of cultivating relationships through thoughtful acts, looking for ways to connect with and surprise people can be very enjoyable. Lifting people's spirits is a gift in today's over-stressed culture.

That's all well and good, yet you may ask, **"Will developing 'my people' have a measurable result?"** Not in the trackable and measurable way you expect from your advertising or marketing efforts. But you will see growth and **multiple benefits to your business as a natural consequence** of consistent and habitual regard and attention to others.

Think about it. If you are conscientious in making referrals yourself, you are likely to prompt referrals of your own. If you acknowledge referrals and other gestures, you will also make it more likely others will respond in kind.

Yet, it's best to do these things without expecting a specific result from a particular person. You're creating a generous, caring atmosphere around yourself and your business. That should be your main focus. Like attracts like. Generosity prompts generosity.

Let's look at this another way. As mentioned before, **developing your network is like farming**.

Farming involves tilling and fertilizing the ground, then planting seeds or young shoots. With sunshine and prudent watering on your part, you'll have a generous harvest of crops, even if you wind up with more zucchini than you expected and less corn.

In other words, **small efforts made consistently over time** will develop your many relationships so you and they gain in unanticipated ways.

This is an entirely different modality than "hunting," which includes more sales-driven finding/sorting/pursuing marketing methods.

We don't object to these methods at all, but cultivating your network has other benefits, as we've discussed in previous chapters. Here are some of the benefits of cultivating your network. . .

- ▸ Access to your contacts' connections – more options
- ▸ Referrals to people totally unknown to you
- ▸ Serendipity that rises naturally out of your relationships
- ▸ Fewer degrees of separation from almost anyone
- ▸ Less isolation because you're actively in touch
- ▸ More social power, as Gladwell noted in *The Tipping Point*

Think about it. Those are benefits – intangible assets – you wouldn't have through any other means than developing relationships of all sorts.

Is it worth the effort? Leading CEOs, political leaders and social mavens would say, "Absolutely." Here, then, are. . .

Simple things that can surprise and delight with little effort and expense.

To get you started, there are some common – and not so common – ideas to surprise people. Their unexpected and personalized nature makes these remembrances special.

This is where **the thought really does count**, and not the amount of money you spend. As a small business owner or independent professional, you can't outspend your larger competitors. But you can make a very real connection when it's clear you made note of certain preferences or simply took the time to make an unexpected contact.

▸ **Send postcards while on vacation.** Perry Marshall, pay-per-click consultant and author of *The Definitive Guide to Google AdWords,* is only one of several relationship-savvy business people to use this friendly touch.

David Frey, founder of Marketing Best Practices, Inc., is another. Obviously, this is a fun way to connect with customers and prospects, as well as colleagues, friends and family.

I mentioned Send Out Cards earlier. You can snap vacation photos or pictures at a business conference, upload them from your laptop and create a personal postcard. Send it to a single individual or a whole group of people while you're still at the beach.

Best of all, you don't have to haul your address book along when the recipients are already in your online database at the Send Out Cards site.

▸ **Photos.** As mentioned in the "Hello" chapter, photos are great connectors. When you're photographed with someone, it freezes a moment when you were together in person, usually at a time everyone is enjoying a good time. The ambiance of that moment can carry over to times long after the event.

Anytime you're able to photograph your colleague or friend with his or her spouse, children or pets, make a print and send it to them in a card (or create a photo card if you use Send Out Cards), with an appropriate message. Or frame it before giving it to them. A person's family – including the dog or cat – shows your respect for the relationships in their lives.

Another good use of photos is to send personal greetings or congratulations to a customer or client. For example, if your customer holds an anniversary celebration, take a photo and create a card with your congratulations. Such thoughtful gestures simply can't be ignored.

▸ **Going to a game, concert or show? Save your program or buy a souvenir**. Who in your network loves Blue Man Group? The Braves? Yo-Yo Ma? If you note who shares your interests in entertainment, you have an opportunity to share your passion, even if they live across the country.

You can buy or beg additional programs if the event is one that several in your network would appreciate. At smaller venues, like clubs, you might be able to get an autograph of the performer(s) for the recipient, making it a true one-of-a-kind remembrance.

▸ **Feed them**. Nothing breaks the ice like chocolate chip cookies or some other fun food everyone can share. All those warm feelings spread through an office.

You don't have to spend a fortune to have impact. If, for example, you know the individual you want to surprise is a chocolate fanatic, a small collection of truffles can have as much impact as a large box of less distinguished candies.

As a side note, Send Out Cards gives you the option to include gourmet gifts, saving you the trouble of shopping, wrapping and mailing a gift.

▸ **Books**. Like Jake, you may want to send the latest business book to a number of people on your list. Many business books are targeted for multiple-copy distribution, and significant discounts can apply.

In addition, keep your ears open to catch the preferences of people on your list. If you hear one of your contacts mention an author, book or topic, you can probably find something that will be an ideal surprise. There are many online sources for new, used, rare and out-of-print books. Here are a few. . .

www.amazon.com   www.bookfinder.com

www.acebooks.com   www.powells.com

If books become a signature item for you, consider having personalized bookmarks designed and printed to slip into each copy.

▶ **Favorite things**. When you deepen your relationships even slightly, you'll learn what leisure activities your contacts enjoy.

Keep your eyes open for small, unusual items related to their interests. To repeat, **the fact that you remembered something that's important to them is truly the gift** – the gift of attention – and the "thing" itself is secondary.

Summary. . .

▶ Developing relationships pays off in good will. A group of people who know and trust you is an intangible asset for you and your business.

▶ Learning to listen for clues to what's important to people is key to being able to surprise them.

▶ Your remembering what's important to them is the gift. What you spend is unimportant.

*The well-timed, thoughtful surprise shows
you care about what's important to the recipient.*

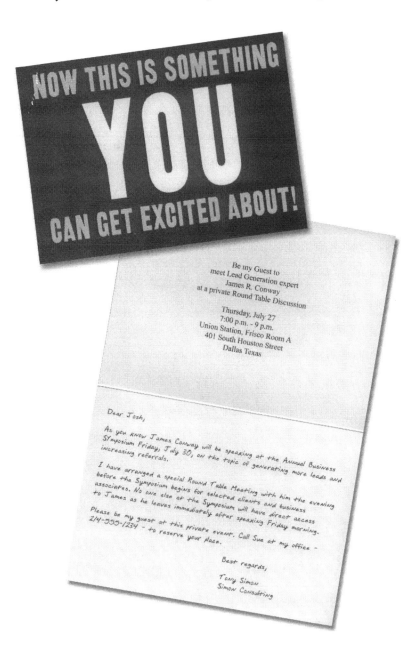

CHAPTER 8

"I'm sorry."

An apology is the superglue of life.
It can repair just about anything.
Lynn Johnston
Creator of the "For Better or For Worse" comic strip

In this Chapter. . .

▸ Why apologies are inevitable and necessary.

▸ How to write an apology that solves the problem.

▸ What you can do in addition to an apology to restore the relationship.

When Dr. Tapas K. Das Gupta (his real name), chairman of surgical oncology at the University of Illinois Medical Center, looked at the X-ray, he realized his mistake. He had removed tissue from the wrong rib. Despite the typical "defend and deny" tactics used by hospitals in such cases, Dr. Das Gupta apologized to the patient and her husband.

The patient's lawyer reported, "She told me that the doctor was completely honest, and so frank that. . . all the anger was gone. . . His apology helped get the case settled for a lower amount."

The hospital instituted a policy of disclosure of medical errors, honest apologies, and fair compensation. According to Dr. Timothy B. McDonald, the hospital's chief safety and risk officer, malpractice filings have dropped by half since the new program was started. Of the 37 cases in which the hospital acknowledged an error and apologized, only one person proceeded with a lawsuit.

("Doctors Say 'I'm Sorry' Before 'See You in Court,'" *New York Times,* May 18, 2008)

• • •

We all make mistakes. There are miscommunications, missed deadlines, poor customer service, faulty products and late deliveries.

There's a seemingly endless list of things that can go wrong between you and your customers or clients, business colleagues, friends, family and acquaintances.

But there is tremendous power in a sincere apology.

Researchers Edward Tomlinson and Roy Lewicki found that people who are wronged in a business transaction may be more likely to say they would reconcile if the offender offers a sincere apology – particularly if the offender takes personal blame for the misdeed.

"The results showed that the victims were much more willing to consider reconciliation when the client offered an explicit apology rather than simply an attempt to placate the victim.

"Moreover, apologies were most effective when the client took personal blame for the situation rather than blaming outside forces.

"'We read in the news all the time stories about CEOs and other leaders who refuse to take responsibility for their actions and refuse to apologize for their offenses,' Lewicki said.

"'But our research suggests a willingness to take blame and offer amends can have a positive effect, and may be necessary to help repair a loss of trust in a business relationship.'"

(*Ohio State University Research News*, http://research-news.osu.edu)

Here's what works and what doesn't work. . .

▸ Don't delay. Time won't make it better and could make it worse, particularly if there are potential legal implications, such as in Dr. Das Gupta's case. Apologize as soon as you realize there's a problem.

▸ Don't lay blame or make excuses. It just makes things worse and stalls a resolution.

▸ Don't argue, particularly with a customer.

▸ Don't quote "policy." It doesn't work with large corporations and it certainly won't play well when you're the boss who made the policy. When a mistake is made, forget policy and figure out what will correct the situation as fast as possible.

▸ Don't "Sorry if. . ." the situation. Some people state the obvious, as if that's enough. "We can't meet your deadline. We're sorry if this causes you any inconvenience."

This makes light of what could cause the customer or client much more than a little inconvenience. There's no respect or responsibility shown to the customer or client in this sideways apology.

▸ Don't try to resolve the issue through e-mail. The chances for further misunderstanding escalate.

▸ Do stay calm and listen in person or by phone if possible. Otherwise you may jump to conclusions about what the real issue is.

▸ Do convey that you want to do whatever is necessary to resolve the issue, because the relationship is important to you.

▸ Do let customers tell you their version of events that brought them to this point. (In other words, let them vent. If you don't, they may feel you're treating them as though they have no cause for upset.)

▸ Do offer positive options. If your options are unacceptable, ask, "What would it take to make this right for you?"

▸ Do resolve the issue and make amends to the other person as soon as possible.

▸ Do match the words, sentiments and formality to the situation and recipient. Attorneys may prefer carefully worded, legally bullet-proof apologies. People prefer a sincere apology from the heart.

British writer G. K. Chesterton understood human nature well when he said,

"A stiff apology is a second insult. . . The injured party does not want to be compensated because he has been wronged; he wants to be healed because he has been hurt."

Somewhere in the process – before or after the resolution of the problem – it's imperative to send a written apology.

Here's a reliable "7-R" approach. . .

1. **Recap** – Outline the details of the problem to clarify.

2. **Responsibility** – Own up to your accountability in the situation that affected the other person.

3. **Recognize** – Acknowledge the hurt or damage that has been done.

4. **Regret** – Express sincere regret.

5. **Reassure** – Explain what steps are being taken to prevent the event from happening again.

6. **Restitution** – Detail how you plan to resolve any damage or loss.

7. **Reconciliation** – Ask for forgiveness.

February, 2007, brought severe weather to the Northeast, Midwest, Florida and Texas. This caused many flight delays and upset customers. JetBlue Airways had a difficult time recovering with both aircraft and personnel in the wrong locations. You'll see in these excerpts elements from 7-Rs above. Many consider this an excellent example of an effective corporate apology.

CEO David Needleman offered a straightforward, unvarnished apology – a corporate mea culpa with more candor than we're used to seeing.

"We are sorry and embarrassed. But most of all, we are deeply sorry. . .

"Words cannot express how truly sorry we are for the anxiety, frustration and inconvenience that you, your family, friends and colleagues experienced. This is especially saddening because JetBlue was founded on the promise of bringing humanity back to air travel. . . We know we failed to deliver on this promise last week.

"We are committed to you, our valued customers, and are taking immediate corrective steps to regain your confidence in us. . . we have published the JetBlue Airways Customer Bill of Rights – our official commitment to you of how we will handle operational interruptions going forward – including details of compensation.

"You deserved better – a lot better – from us last week and we let you down. Nothing is more important than regaining your trust. . ."

Not many of us are thrilled to travel by air today, regardless of the airline. Yet we have to wonder, did the apology work?

A few sources dismissed his apology as so much corporate smoke, yet many praised it for the admission of responsibility and sincere regret. In the wake of many other CEOs who routinely sidestep responsibility, Needleman stepped up.

As of April 2009, Sky Trax (http://www.airlinequality.com), which posts consumer reviews, shows JetBlue at a commendable 4-Star rating out of five stars.

Here's how a company might use the 7-Rs in an apology for less catastrophic problems. . .

Dear Mr. Johnson,

Please accept my apology once again for the problem you had during your last visit to the dealership for repairs.

After your phone call, I spoke to our service manager, Mike Benson, to find out why your car wasn't ready on time. When you checked your car in, the computer indicated the part needed was in stock.

Mike later learned that the computer inventory had not been updated the previous evening and the part had to be ordered.

Due to a breakdown in communications within the shop, you were not alerted. The error was entirely our fault, and we regret the inconvenience we caused you and your family.

Your car was repaired the following day and, as promised, we drove it to your office so you wouldn't need to be driven to our location a second time.

My staff and I sincerely want you to know that we value your business and are truly sorry for any inconvenience or upset that we caused you.

I've enclosed both a certificate for $25 off any future service and a $15 gas card to compensate you for the needless roundtrip drive.

We trust this resolves the problem we caused to your satisfaction and that you'll allow us to serve you again in the future.

Best regards,

Joe Blackwell
Blackwell Motors

Handling a "tiny" mistake. . .

What should you do if you made a mistake, a *faux pas*, or some error that didn't do much harm, but would reflect poorly on you or your team?

Terrie Williams suggests in *The Personal Touch* a "little humble pie" in the form of a "happily" letter. Here's how she uses it. . .

"Happily, it's not often that we must send a letter such as this. But when required, we do so with a sense of duty. . ."

She says cleaning up small, embarrassing blunders such as misspelled names or typos "separates us from others."

Saying "I'm sorry" in your personal relationships.

Because this book is about building relationships in **all five relationship circles**, it's important to know how to say you're sorry in tangible ways. Among friends and colleagues, consider something extra to include with your note of apology. . .

▸ **Flowers.** Yes, flowers are still a classic, save-face, I'm-so-sorry solution between friends and family members. You probably already know florists can make arrangements suitable for men as well as women.

▸ **Lunch.** If the infraction is serious enough, things may be resolved more easily face-to-face over lunch. Apologize first, then use the lunch as an event to reconcile one-on-one and repair any damage that was done to the relationship and restore the warmth.

▸ **A greeting card.** Often, the graphics and sentiments of a greeting card can express your apologies very effectively. Personal mail is so rare these days that a hand-addressed, stamped envelope will say repairing the problem is worth taking the time to mail a card.

Send Out Cards lets you get an apology out quickly, with no hassle. If you put off making an apology, things will only get worse.

▶ **A book, CD or DVD.** A favorite buddy movie or chick flick, a book of poetry or music from a favorite performer can mend fences and heal wounds among close associates, friends or family members.

Being humble enough to apologize, even if you feel you're in the right, is often sufficient to calm even the most irate person who feels wronged by you or your employees.

When "I'm sorry" is an expression of sympathy or shared sorrow for a loss. . .

When there's **a death in the family** of anyone you know, a card or note is always appreciated. Like many other communications, how you express your sympathy will be tempered by how well you know the individual.

Finding the right words is often difficult, which is why a tasteful card is a better choice than wrestling with what to say and then doing nothing.

Don't be tempted to send an e-mail sympathy card. Unless your only contact information for someone is an e-mail address, mail a real card. (It's a rare household or office that has a supply of sympathy cards on hand. Your card can be on the way quickly if you use Send Out Cards.)

It's thoughtful to send a "thinking of you" note of support in the weeks following the funeral, as many people feel completely isolated after a death.

There are other kinds of losses, however. When someone has lost a job, a family member has been diagnosed with a major illness, or there's been a divorce or breakdown of a relationship. . . respond according to the level of your relationship.

When people are in distress, we sometimes tend to give advice when what they need is quiet support. If their status has changed, they may think your opinion about them has changed. When in doubt, say little. "I'm so sorry. . ." is often all that's needed for them to know you care.

Summary. . .

▶ Act quickly when you know – or as soon as you find out – someone has been harmed or hurt due to some action or inaction on your part.

▶ If someone feels wronged, it's emotional. You can't explain it away with logic. Apologize. Then make things right.

▶ Only a sincere apology will bridge the gap. Avoid the unapologetic sidestepping used by large corporations and politicians.

▶ "I'm sorry" also means sharing in the sorrow of others. We're all in this together.

*A sincere apology is the one gesture
that can repair a relationship quickly.*

Dear Mrs Hamilton,

I was very disturbed to hear you were disappointed with the service you received during your recent visit to the spa. I am so sorry.

A key employee was called away due to a family emergency that day. Despite their best efforts, the remaining staff didn't deliver the level of service you have come to expect from us.

Please accept my apologies, as well as an invitation to return for a complimentary massage and pedicure at your convenience.

Sincerely,

Jo Beth Anderson

CHAPTER 9

"Thought you'd be interested in this."

*You can make more friends in two months
by becoming more interested in other people
than you can in two years
by trying to get people interested in you.*
Dale Carnegie

In this Chapter. . .

▶ Why attention to what's interesting to others builds solid relationships.

▶ How to show that you're genuinely interested in others and not what's in it for you.

▶ What encouraging words can do to build any relationship, business or personal.

Joanne was an interior designer whose business relied on happy clients who referred their friends. However, because she only handled a few clients at a time, the overall number of referrals was small. In some cases, interested prospects had to move more quickly than she could accommodate them.

She contacted Brendan, a successful colleague in another city, who advised her to immediately start a program of staying in touch with people in her network, other than customers.

He told her, "Referrals can pop up from the most unusual and unexpected places." Brendan noted that he'd landed a large commercial project through an unlikely source: his pool man.

Brendan passed along his strategy: find out what's of specific interest to people to show you've paid attention to what they said when talking with them.

Joanne was an avid reader who kept current in general news and trends, as well as publications and online newsletters in her own and related fields. She used her own interests to build bridges to others with similar tastes.

Her first goal was to send one item a day to someone on her list. These included articles torn from magazines, e-mails with links to specific articles, and even notices of workshops she knew certain people would be enjoy.

To her surprise, after a few months, she did hear from people regarding referrals. More surprising, however, were other unexpected calls. She was invited to speak at a luncheon of CEOs about the influence of design in office environments, particularly on employee morale and productivity.

In addition, someone recommended her as one of the guest designers to create a room for a local charity's "Show House" fundraiser. Joanne also met a new supplier for custom-made, hand-carved beds.

Her first-year efforts were so rewarding, both personally and professionally, that she turned more attention to listening attentively to people so she could become a better source of information.

◆ ◆ ◆

In this chapter, you'll hear echoes from previous chapters – particularly "Hello" and "Your Five Relationship Circles."

One of the most direct routes to connecting with another individual is to **listen, pay attention, and take note** of the things that are important to them. Once you know some areas that are of special importance – whether it's golf, bagpipes, organic vegetables or astronomy – you have a basis for connection that can truly deepen the relationship.

When you've uncovered one or two interests of people in any of your circles, then what?

> ▸ Virtually every contact management system has a place to make notes about people. You can go beyond "prospect" or "client" and identify a person as a golfer, health nut, or other subgroup.

If you can pull up a list of all your golfers, it'll make your contacts personal, but also efficient, when you find information unique to their interest.

▶ Over time, add new information *as you discover it naturally*. Today, no one is going to give you much more than superficial personal information until they get to know you and trust you. Gradually you'll learn the dog's name. You'll find out they collect hand-tied fishing lures or discover a favorite genre of movies.

▶ Keep your communications at a level that's appropriate for the relationship. Getting too personal too fast can have a decidedly creepy, intrusive feel to it. Keep things light. Follow their lead.

▶ Use your knowledge of the recipient's interest sparingly. Better to send one incredible White Paper with break-through information than a dozen generic blurbs. These items are "extra" contacts you add to your thank-you notes and other communications.

But what should I send?
How should I send it?

Not knowing what to send is the greatest barrier to people making the effort.

Your choices for delivery are simple and obvious. This type of contact requires no more special treatment than all your normal, everyday correspondence.

▶ If you already have an **e-mail relationship** with the person, it's likely your e-mail and any attachment will be opened.

▶ If you're sending a clipping or magazine article, **mail it with a personal note** or just a Post-it® Note. You can almost guarantee that it will be opened.

▶ You can **deliver it in person** if you see the individual at work or in social situations.

What you send is limited only to the types of things you normally come across that you might share. . .

- ▸ **Links** are simple and convenient for you and the recipient. As mentioned earlier, news sites and other information sources routinely have "e-mail this" options so the link is sent by the publication.

  When you discover an obscure link, just copy and sent it by e-mail with your brief message.

  Two of the great, lighthearted resources online are written by Randy Cassingham – www.thisistrue.com with what he calls "weird news" and www.thestellaawards.com, which is the true Stella awards based on research of strange court cases.

  Each has a free subscription option, although Randy encourages you to upgrade to the premium edition of *This is True* once you can't resist his weekly take on the news. There are also video editions now. All shareable.

  Also, Randy has a feature in *This is True*, "Bonzer Site of the Week," which highlights some very useful sites you never knew existed that you also might want to share.

- ▸ **Magazine articles and news clippings** are exchanged routinely among colleagues and friends. Keep your radar up for intriguing or noteworthy items.

- ▸ **Resources** are good to share. For example, if you're on a plane and see the exact widget you know someone is looking for in the SkyMall catalog, stash the catalog in your briefcase.

  Other resources include referrals to people in your network or your network's networks. Finding reliable resources is the whole point behind the various business social network connection sites – LinkedIn, Plaxo, etc.

- ▸ **Upcoming events, workshops, seminars, and performances** are welcome, especially if the person who'd appreciate it would not necessarily have seen the announcement or ad.

These are the most common topical items to send, which gives you several simple ways to start. You're reading the paper anyway. You're cruising the Internet. You're flipping through catalogs. Simply hold the question in mind, "Who do I know that would find this interesting?"

It's an excellent way to provide value to anyone whose interests are known to you, but particularly to business colleagues.

Does this sound too simple? The strength of this form of contact is that it truly is personal. It will have impact. Yes, even if they saw the article or visited the Web site previously.

To summarize, there are only two things required to make this powerful relationship-builder work:

1. You must have some personal contact with the individual so you can identify one or more areas that are of interest.

2. You need to be willing to have some part of your brain scanning for things that will please the recipients and show your attention.

Please note: Not everyone on your list is going to qualify for this one-on-one treatment. Start with your core list and expand the number of people you include over time.

Positive and encouraging words build relationships.

An option that doesn't require deep knowledge of an individual's interests is to send great, positive – sometimes funny – quotes. Great quotes provide insights and address issues we all face.

For example, business owners respond to quotes about tenacity, money, service and integrity. Friends and acquaintances are uplifted by inspirational quotes or wry humorous quotes about life.

In a down economy, positive messages are always welcome. In an up economy, encouraging words can lift a person who's having a tough day.

Where to find good quotes.

We have many quote books in our library, but we now usually search online. There are many excellent sites that have quotes on virtually any topic.

In Google, I normally put the word "quotations" in the search box followed by the topic, such as "business" or "money." You can also add "motivational" or "inspirational" to your search.

We also pull quotes from magazine articles, blogs, online quotation sites, newsletters and books we read. Quotes from famous or not-so-famous people writing today can be right on target, especially regarding current economic conditions or experiences that people can relate to easily.

How to use quotes.

Great quotations that uplift and inspire can be sent to multiple people in your various relationship circles.

You can also stage a personal campaign to help someone you know – customer, colleague or friend – through a tough time you're privy to without getting too personal or prying into their business.

We had a client who went through a series of incredibly difficult circumstances that crashed around him like dominoes. Unraveling it all took years. The man has grit and the mental discipline to feed his mind on the positive. He worked through each step required to turn things right again, combating the negatives with optimism and hope.

As the final resolution of his catastrophic problems was in view, there were a few more unexpected obstacles to overcome. We stopped sending "How are you doing" e-mails and replaced them with quotations. The subject lines would read, "As Winston Churchill said. . ."

When we spoke to him after a particularly grueling week, we asked what we could do to support him through the last hurdles. He said, "Keep sending the quotes."

If you use Send Out Cards, you can set up customized quote cards that will be ready for you to use any time. This is the kind of unexpected mail that can really make a difference if you know a customer or client, friend or family member could use a lift.

In business and in life, you can't go wrong being the bearer of the uplifting and the positive. Injecting even a few moments of inspiration, motivation or humor can help turn a bad day right again.

Summary. . .

▸ Showing interest in another person by noting what's important to them is flattering and relatively uncommon in business today.

▸ Sending information or resources for their hobbies or interests is a tangible way to show your attention and respect.

▸ Providing timely, worthwhile information to those on your business list can help you develop trust and credibility among prospects and customers, as well as colleagues.

▸ Using motivational, inspirational or humorous quotations can give a lift to anyone, any time.

Sending well-chosen resources and information to someone says "I was thinking about you." That's what builds relationships.

CHAPTER 10

"Congratulations!"

Because we live in a fast-paced, often impersonal era, it's more critical than ever to offer the little niceties that might easily be forgotten, yet make others feel important or appreciated.
Jacqueline Whitmore, *Business Class*

In this Chapter. . .

▸ Why celebrating someone else's victories and milestones is important for your own success.

▸ How to convey your congratulations.

▸ What to do to make an exciting event even more memorable for someone you know.

Dan was a hard worker in the highly competitive insurance field. Although he was a high achiever, he wasn't in the elite top group. . . yet. Even so, every time a representative at his company was recognized, which could occur for monthly, quarterly or annual achievements, Dan made a point of sending a note of congratulations.

His wife thought he was nuts. "Your co-workers are really competitive. I don't hear them praising you for your achievements. What's in it for you, Dan?"

He replied in a matter-of-fact manner: "We're in a tough business, Jane. When someone excels, it raises the bar for all of us. We get knocked down so often, we have to celebrate when one of us overcomes the obstacles and scores a win.

"Don't you see, Jane, if one of us can hit a new high mark, that's available to all of us. If I don't cheer him on, it's as though I'm not cheering myself on to higher performance. If I withhold praise for him, I'm setting up a limitation for myself. Can't you see that?"

It was true that Dan didn't get congratulations from many of the others in his group. A few would clap him on the back after a meeting where he was honored, but other than a couple of e-mails from his sales manager, he didn't get – or expect – recognition from his peers.

"I'm doing this for me as much as for them," he would say.

Dan never did hit the Number 1 spot in the sales department, but he did very well by producing solid, steady sales over time. When the sales manager, Nathan, moved to another firm to accept a vice president's position, Dan immediately sent a personal note of congratulations. To his surprise, Nathan called.

"Dan, I want you to come over here to work with me in management," he said before highlighting the financial incentives. Dan couldn't help but wonder silently why Nathan had called him instead of his high-performance colleagues. Nathan answered his unasked question candidly.

"Dan, I like your style. Always have. The courtesy and professionalism you showed in consistently supporting the other sales reps let me know you'll do well with our clientele. Selling is one thing. Class is another thing altogether. The executives here put stock in building long-term relationships. You'll fit in well."

◆ ◆ ◆

In a high-tech world, people in general need high-touch attention. People can get away with marginal manners when they're in low-level jobs. But the higher they climb as their careers develop, the greater the need for good manners and social graces that are largely absent from our culture.

When do you send congratulations?

When you get into the habit of sending congratulations, you're going to be looking for excuses to send them, especially if you use Send Out Cards to make it easy and convenient. The list below consists of the obvious and some less obvious opportunities to congratulate someone who has reason to celebrate.

This is a category of correspondence that applies to all five of your **relationship circles**. . .

1. **Customers or clients** – After a while, you'll get to know at least some of your clients and customers on a more personal level, and possibly even their spouses, children, and pets. Business and personal milestones are fair game, depending on the nature and closeness of your relationship.

   Even the most formal relationships allow for congratulations when the customer or client is promoted or recognized by a professional or charitable organization for service.

2. **Prospects** – Again, unless developing a prospect is a long process, you won't know about many events that call for congratulations. However, if you hear of a promotion, take the opportunity to send a note if the level of your relationship and contact would make it natural.

3. **Business associates** – You're only limited by the number of celebratory occasions you can discover – a promotion, new job, new account, engagement, wedding, new baby, new must-have electronic gadget.

4. **Friends & family** – Any reason will do: engagements, weddings, graduations, promotions, new home, new dog, new car, new plasma TV. The opportunities are wide open in this group.

5. **Acquaintances** – You may not know of many occasions to send congratulations to this group. But when you discover a reason, use the opportunity to make a personal, high-touch contact.

Many people save the written notes and cards they receive at a special event. Your note or card may be saved, only to be unpacked and enjoyed again years later.

You don't send congratulations as a gimmick to trigger sales or referrals, but to build cordial relationships. However, when you make a habit of sending congratulations when few others make the gesture, you enter the "know, like, trust... and remember" group most likely to get new business and referrals.

Beyond the note. . .
making your congratulations memorable.

If the relationship itself calls for you, personally, to make a very big deal about the occasion, you may want to do more than a card or note. . .

▸ **Send flowers, a plant, a fruit basket or balloons.** These are the universal staples of celebrations.

▸ **Take the one honored to lunch.** Organize a group lunch with friends or co-workers to celebrate.

▸ **Find the news clipping** or photo about the achievement or award. Clip it out, and have it framed.

▸ **Snap a picture** at the presentation. Have it framed with a caption of the event.

▸ **Commission a local awards company to create a commemorative plaque** or trophy to mark the event. Although plaques are often serious, yours doesn't have to be.

And one final note – if a person hasn't been recognized for anything special, look for a way to honor and recognize him or her – or a whole team.

Many people's important contributions are made behind the scenes, without fanfare or notice. There are no ceremonies. There are few congratulations for a job well done. In these cases, offering congratulations and recognition is a version of appreciation.

At an agency where I consulted, our team met and exceeded projections on a difficult client-retention assignment. The client company treated the entire group – including the account service people and creative team – to an afternoon at an amusement park, where we crashed bumper cars into each other and wallowed in junk food.

After endless months of nose-to-grindstone work, we couldn't have felt more appreciated for our efforts.

Summary. . .

▶ Look for opportunities to offer your congratulations. It won't diminish you or your achievements, and in fact enhances your professionalism.

▶ Sending a congratulatory note, or making a big splash over a particularly important achievement or milestone, is rare today. Making it a habit can set you apart.

▶ Don't forget those who aren't in the front lines where awards and recognition are passed out liberally. There are often behind-the-scenes efforts that deserve recognition, celebration and congratulations. Attention counts.

*Celebration of others' victories, successes and accomplishments
signals that what's important to them is important to you.*

CHAPTER 11

"Happy Birthday!"

*There are three hundred and sixty-four days
when you might get un-birthday presents. . .
and only one for birthday presents, you know.*
Lewis Carroll

~~~~~~

In this Chapter. . .

▸ Why everyone enjoys receiving a birthday card.

▸ How un-birthday cards can add sparkle to the lives of anyone in your five relationship circles.

▸ What are the wrong ways to do birthday cards for business contacts?

~~~~~~

This is a true story from Send Out Cards. Laurel was at a trade show where Jeff was exhibiting the SOC system. As he held the door for her, he noticed she was dragging a bit, so he struck up a conversation with her.

When he asked why she was there, she said she was looking at all the opportunities at the show. He took her name and birth date. When Laurel's birthday rolled around, Jeff sent her a card.

On her 50th birthday, Laurel went to her mail box. There was one card in the box. From Jeff. "It was the only card," she said with tears glistening in her eyes, ". . . that I could hold in my hand."

◆ ◆ ◆

How important are birthday cards? We say, "Very!" Today, we assume that everyone has plenty of people to send them greetings. And they may have plenty of friends, family and business colleagues. Yet most people are under-celebrated for their birthdays.

You can make a very big difference in people's lives – and in your relationship with them – if you are thoughtful enough to send a card. In the real-life story of Laurel, her disappointment was that Jeff's card was the only card she could actually hold. And, by the way, the only card she could tuck away to commemorate her milestone 50th birthday.

Perhaps you're one of those hardy, no-nonsense folks who breezes through birthdays without a thought. "Never give it a thought," you say. Well, the rest of the world isn't so well armored or self-sufficient that being forgotten on a birthday doesn't sting, if just a little.

That's why sending birthday cards to everyone – really, *everyone... EVERY ONE* – in your five relationship circles is one of The Most Important Things You Can Do To Build Relationships. Period. End of paragraph.

Candidly, I'd advise you to be in contact on other occasions also, but don't miss the birthdays.

Why is this so? Because probably everyone else has forgotten. Or at best, the people on the "must remember list," such as Mom or a brother, may be the only ones who celebrate.

> "Psychologists tell us that most people identify with and respond strongly to their own name. People also respond strongly to anything that has to do with their birthday. It's a very special day for most people (despite what someone might say about how it's just 'another day older')..." ("Birthday Marketing Can Rev Up Your Business," www.nfib.com).

A simple birthday card can turn a friendly acquaintance into a friend. . . a friend into a good friend.

Now, will it turn a prospect into a customer? Not likely. Will it cause a customer to run down to your store and shop? Also not likely. But the recipient will smile if you don't goof up this important relationship opportunity.

What? You can goof up a birthday card to a customer? Oh, yes you can.

Don't let your birthday greetings backfire.

Let me give you a real-life example. I have an IRA with a well-known firm. When I opened the account, I was living just minutes from the local office and had a "friendly acquaintance" with the agent.

When we moved, I soon was shuffled off to a new agent I'd never met. She never called to see if my financial goals had changed... or even to get acquainted when she got my file. Yet, on my birthday, she sent a card that felt very much like a perfunctory greeting.

A year later, again with no contact regarding my account with the firm, I received another card signed cheerily by the agent and some other person I'd never heard of. Lew happened to know it was a new assistant. Yet another person I've never been introduced to or communicated with in any way.

Instead of making me smile, these greetings are having the exact opposite effect on me.

As a financial advisor, she would be smart to actually tend to my business relationship. This doesn't feel warm to me at all. Or friendly. Or cheery. I'm a customer. Please pay some attention to me when it counts. The card only reminds me that you've ignored me completely for another whole year.

This year, I received a card prior to my birthday that read, "You're not just getting older. . ." and candidly, I don't know what the rest of the headline said. The card was a soft promotion for some financial product a smart person would be interested in.

The quote this copy is based on is the iconic slogan that debuted for Loving Care hair color in 1971: "You're not getting older. You're getting better." Nice. I like that.

But with the questionable take off, "You're not *just* getting older," I stopped cold. Really? Thanks. I hadn't thought about it. What else is happening besides my aging that you noticed?

I will now step down off my soapbox, because you can see how easily birthday cards for customers that are a "stand alone" marketing and relationship strategy are just inadequate. They may even work against you with customers or clients.

These things trouble me, but in fairness, when it comes to how a customer is handled, I'm looking for gaps, holes and missteps. That's my job.

With all our clients, I am the voice of the customer. I review what the client is doing and give a blow-by-blow account of how each customer contact – from the Web site to how the phone is answered – is likely to make the customer feel.

You may not subscribe to the theory that feelings enter the picture in business. But the simple truth is, how people feel about you, your company, and your products or services trumps almost everything else. Bean counters may disagree, but it's true.

That's why I also question the common "wisdom" of sending a customer a discount coupon to celebrate their birthday. Come on. To get a small birthday acknowledgement I have to spend money with you? Well, happy birthday to me, I think I'll just keep my money in my pocket.

Please do not contact me on my birthday if you're trying to sell me products.

Let's say you own a spa. You have access to many products in small, even sample, sizes. Why not create a small gift bag with several wonderful products and just give it to your customer? For the most impact, mail the gift. Otherwise, send a card and write a note inside that says, "I have a gift here with your name on it waiting until the next time you come in."

If you've always sent a discount coupon and you have positive feedback from your customers, then continue it, but add a small gift anyway that's not attached to any "deal."

Now, let's say you own a restaurant. On my birthday, I get a free lunch or dinner. Some restaurants want you to bring at least one other person. More likely I'll show up with my usual lunch crowd or my entire family for dinner. Plus, I'll get to be embarrassed by a bunch of strangers singing to celebrate my birthday, and enjoy a free dessert with a candle stuck on top.

Do you have to buy to get the free meal? There probably is a purchase in the mix somewhere, but you're going out anyway, right? It has a different and decidedly more festive feel. This is a common and well-accepted offer at casual dining restaurants.

Imagine you're **in a business that doesn't normally give birthday greetings** or gifts. You have a special opportunity to make an impression if no one else in your industry bothers.

Let's say you own an auto repair shop. It's unlikely you're going to offer a discount on an oil change. You already distribute coupons for those to customers. And rotating tires isn't quite the thing either. But what if you gave your customers an auto- or travel-related birthday gift? Be with them every morning when they commute. Accompany your customer on vacation and business trips.

Let's think this through together. A travel mug. Yes, with your company name on it. A laminated city map. A quality tire gauge. A small LED flashlight. All you need is a little imagination.

How to surprise someone with an un-birthday or half-birthday.

Soon you'll be famous for sending birthday cards. Upgrade to include un-birthdays and half-birthdays.

- **Un-birthdays,** in case you've forgotten, are the 364 days (365 in leap years) that are not the recipient's actual birthday. The Happy Un-birthday song was first heard in Disney's animated classic, *Alice in Wonderland.* YouTube has several videos of it, if you need a little reminder.

  This gives you a reason for celebrating any day of the year other than a person's actual birthday. If you're going to tie a sales event to a birthday theme, it's better to use the un-birthday than the real birthday. It won't seem quite so crass and it's "un-usual."

  If you're fresh out of things to send, an un-birthday card can come to your rescue.

- **Half-birthdays** are exactly six months between birthdays. It's one more opportunity for a friendly greeting. It has the added benefit of being un-expected.

How to manage your birthday greetings.

Lew and I used to spend hours shopping for birthday cards to have on hand. Unfortunately, we often missed the mailing date to get a card to the recipient on time. And, as you know, the price of cards has shot through the roof.

That's why we find Send Out Cards to be such an elegant solution. You open an account with a minimum amount "on account" to cover the cost of a supply of cards and postage. You add more to your balance as necessary.

Once that's done, you simply choose the recipient, pick a card, personalize the message and send. The service prints the card and inserts it in an envelope, adds the stamp, and mails it for you.

Another benefit is convenience. You get a daily reminder of the cards to send that day. (No more forgotten birthdays and anniversaries.)

Is it worth the time and effort?

All businesses are "people" businesses. Sales, good word of mouth and referrals are natural outcomes of building relationships through such simple gestures as sending birthday cards. The primary benefit is for the recipient, and it's one more touch that can help you bond with people and stay top-of-mind.

Summary. . .

▸ Don't ignore birthdays in any of your circles of relationships. You may be only one of a few people who remember a person's special day.

▸ Use un-birthdays and half-birthdays as additional reasons for lighthearted greetings.

▸ Real cards sent by mail cut through the clutter and can make someone's day, and that can make you memorable to them.

Everyone enjoys being remembered on their birthday.

Who can resist a thoughtful, unexpected gift?

CHAPTER 12

"Have a special day!"

Every day's a holiday. . . twice on Sunday.
Jack Windle

In this Chapter. . .

▸ How holidays, anniversaries, and celebrations that commemorate almost any event provide you with endless reasons to stay in touch.

▸ Why fresh and original "special day" greetings are important to building your relationships.

▸ How an attitude of "every day's a holiday" can infuse your business with an uncommon level of enjoyment for everyone.

Jean headed a young, aggressive legal firm with nine employees, counting support staff. With their niche market of helping tax-challenged small businesses, they enjoyed steady growth.

She felt insulated from competition from larger firms, because she'd researched her market and none of the local legal firms courted small businesses. That is, until they noticed her success. Plus, clients also discovered lawyers out of the geographic area on the Internet.

When business leveled off, she sat down with her staff to brainstorm some strategies to reestablish themselves as the leaders in tax problems.

One of the insights that came up from, oddly, the receptionist, was that people were so frightened and tense. Of course, it made sense. The people who came to Jean's firm were terrified. They might put on a brave face to the lawyers, but the receptionist picked up on the cues.

"It's little things they say when they call or are sitting in the lobby waiting for their appointment," Andrea, the receptionist, reported.

"Like what?" Jean thought it was impossible that a receptionist would notice something the lawyers wouldn't spot.

"Well," she said, hesitating and unsure, "One guy said he just felt like he was under a black cloud. His face was all scrunched up. It didn't look like he'd smiled in weeks. It looked to me like he could use a good laugh.

"And your new client, Mr. Simon? Did you know he had gone to Mason & Hopkins first?" That was news to Jean. "He said they made him feel dumb and small. And even though he went to them because he thought it'd be good to have a big company behind him going up against the IRS, he got the impression they considered small businesses like his to be small potatoes."

Jean couldn't resist the obvious question. "How did you get him to tell you all that?"

"Well, I always get the clients coffee while they're waiting, like you said to do. And I try to be nice to anyone who comes in the office and put them at ease. He said they just left him sitting at Mason & Hopkins while they ushered in their corporate clients and treated them like they were important."

Others then retold what client and prospective clients were saying and a picture emerged. Unbeknownst to Jean, besides the firm's top reputation, small businesses came to her company for two additional reasons that were completely invisible to her.

First, clients felt like their team was knowledgeable and scrappy. They talked and acted like bulldogs and were willing to go to the mat for their small business clients. This was different than the experience of clients at the larger firms where they felt the lawyer would do what was required, but wasn't invested in the result.

The staff determined to emphasize their "fight for the little guy" attitude in all their dealings with the clients.

The second reason was that, even though the work was serious, the people were nice, even lighthearted at Jean's firm. That actually lifted the spirits of the clients, not to mention the employees.

Jean and her staff decided to capitalize on this. When anyone called, even to inquire about their services, they were put on the mailing list. Every few weeks they received an e-mail or postcard with an unbelievable tax fact followed by a short, humorous comment.

For example, one postcard carried this message: *In 1916 Congress deleted the word "lawful" before the word "income," making illegal income taxable. This paved the way in one case for IRS agents to use a high-priced call girl's laundry bill to determine how many sheets she sent to the laundry to compute the number of her client, um, meetings and her taxable income. It appears some people would be better off airing their dirty laundry than sending it to be cleaned. Have a great day.*

These messages helped diffuse the anxiety by providing a sense of the absurd. Their clients were not alone. Some clients actually requested that they continue to get the e-mails and postcards even after their cases were cleared.

• • •

The technique Jean used intuitively to lighten the grim and often long-term stress of dealing with the IRS is an unusual version of what Lew and I call the "everyday's a holiday" mailings. All that means is that you can turn any day into a special day for someone with a short, lighthearted message.

These mailings are excellent ways to keep in touch with anyone in your five relationship circles, even your acquaintances.

Here are the types of messages that fall into this category. . .

▸ Actual holiday greetings. Here are the "Official" holidays as stipulated by the U.S. Government. . .

New Year's Day – January 1 every year
Martin Luther King Day – 3rd Monday in January
Inauguration Day – every 4th year, January 20
Presidents Day – 3rd Monday in February
Memorial Day – last Monday in May
Independence Day – July 4 every year
Labor Day – 1st Monday in September

Columbus Day – 2nd Monday in October
Veterans' Day – November 11 every year
Thanksgiving Day – 4th Thursday in November
Christmas Day – December 25 every year

Lew and I often joke that you can instantly tell who's a small business owner and who has a job. All you have to ask is, "So, what are you doing for the holiday?" Employees will tell you their plans. Small business owners will say, "What holiday?"

This opens still another door to make contact with other business owners; "I figured you'd be working today, too, so I thought I'd just wish you a Happy Holiday. Turn off your computer and go relax."

▸ Greetings for "Traditional" holidays.

Valentine's Day – February 14
St. Patrick's Day – March 17
Administrative Professionals Day –
    Wednesday of the last full week of April
Easter – date varies
Mother's Day – Second Sunday in May
Flag Day – June 14
Father's Day – Third Sunday in June
National Bosses Day – October 16
United Nation's Day – October 24
Halloween – October 31

▸ Borrow holidays from other countries.

France – Bastille Day – July 14 marks the
    end of monarchy, the beginning of democracy
Germany – Oktoberfest – October – dates vary
Japan has many colorful holidays, including
    Respect for the Aged Day – September 15
    (what could you do with that one?)
Health and Sports Day – 2nd Monday in October
Sweden – St. Lucia's Day – December 13

▸ Celebrity Birthdays – easy to find online

Elvis – January 8
Bill Gates – October 28
Angelina Jolie – June 4
(You get the idea.)

▸ Choose historic days in your industry.

▸ Celebrate goofy food holidays. Normally promoted by food producers or trade associations, these "National Months," "Weeks" or "Days" provide the foundation for some delightful and off-beat greetings.

National Prune Breakfast Month – January
National Pizza Week – 2nd week of January
Bittersweet Chocolate Day – January 10
National Sticky Bun Day – February 21
Chocolate Chip Cookie Week – 2nd week of March
National Peanut Butter and Jelly Day – April 2

And so on through the year. Search engines will uncover your personal favorites (Nutty Fudge Day? National French Fries Day?).

What's in it for recipients? Or you?

Work can become pretty intense. A little levity can bring some relief into an otherwise dull or overloaded day. It's good for the recipients. It's good for you. Being the dispenser of good cheer makes your presence a welcome one.

Think about the people who feed you all the gloom and doom news, rumors and bad reports. Do you enjoy having them around?

What's great about the holiday and off-holiday greetings is that they give you almost endless opportunities to stay in touch.

The strategy outlined in this book recommends that you keep in touch on a regular basis to build your relationships in all five relationship circles. Many of these people will be among the "weak ties" that are known to be a good source of connections for all of us who run our own businesses.

That means, on your list, you'll have quite a number of people who need a light touch every month or every quarter.

While your customers are on the front burner, these others will be on the back burner. You don't want them to go cold, so you keep just a little heat under them and stir the pot from time to time. It's another way to connect with people and stay on the radar of those who may buy from you or make referrals.

Summary. . .

▶ Holidays and goofy quasi-holidays give you an almost unending source of reasons for you to stay in touch.

▶ Creating good cheer generates good will.

▶ Search engines make it easy to research and write your own messages.

▶ Keeping contacts warm increases the likelihood that recipients will think of you when buying or making recommendations.

A little light-hearted fun goes a long way toward keeping even casual relationships warm.

Lucky You

Happy St. Patrick's Day!

May your blessing outnumber the shamrocks that grow. And may trouble avoid you wherever you go.

Lucky us to know you!

Sandy and Jim

"In sales, a referral is the key to the door of resistance."

Bo Bennett

APPENDIX

Sample Plans for Your Perpetual Contact System™

Skill is fine, and genius is splendid,
but the right contacts are more valuable than either.
Arthur Conan Doyle, Sr.

In this Section. . .

‣ What to include in your plan.

‣ How planning ahead can make Perpetual Contact easy to implement.

‣ Why it's important to include all groups in your Perpetual Contact strategy.

Larry had retired from engineering and pursued his hobby, jewelry making, full-time in his shop, Silver Junction. Like his fellow retailers in the quaint historic shopping district, he experienced seasonal highs and lows.

His customers ooh-ed and ah-ed over his beautifully crafted silver bracelets, belt buckles, rings and earrings during tourist season, but when the season ended, customers evaporated. He had a Web site, but hadn't figured out how to drive traffic to it affordably.

His financial concerns weighed heavily on him. While he could live on retirement funds, he had counted on making a decent living in the attractive town in the southwest so he and his wife could leave the shop in the hands of an employee while they traveled.

As the season closed, his wife, Helen, took home the big leather-covered guest book. "Larry, why don't I put these names into the computer and we'll stay in touch with the shoppers and customers in the off season?"

Although he had collected names, addresses, and e-mail addresses for four years, he had never contacted a single person. A few called the shop for a gift now and then, but he hadn't sent any e-mails or done any mailings at all.

"What would we send them?" he asked. Helen had spent hours in the store while Larry was busy making jewelry pieces. She had heard the comments customers made and had a plan.

"Everyone who comes to our part of the country wants to stay. And even people who don't buy your jewelry are impressed with your designs. What if we give them a sense of what it's like to be here during different parts of the year?"

"How?"

"Well, in October, we could snap a picture and put it on a postcard and just send it out with a 'wish you were here' message. And at Christmas, we could create a custom card to send everyone.

"We don't have everyone's birth date, but we have some. We could send cards with you, me and the dog standing at Lookout Point, which is a view tourists love."

Larry looked skeptical. "This could get expensive."

"Not so much. We could send an e-mail inviting them to our Web site, showing your new designs in time for holiday buying. And we could send another right after Christmas with a clearance sale," she continued. It was obvious she'd given this some thought.

"In between times, I could write a little *Silver Junction Gazette* reporting on local events so people feel they're actually here and part of the community even though they're back home."

She also planned to include educational information about how silver is mined, refined and crafted, plus a special offer for readers.

And just like that, Helen laid out her plan to contact their entire list, including those who bought and those who just dropped by to watch Larry work on the meticulously crafted silver pieces or wander around the store.

She charted out which mailing would go out each month. Intuitively, she knew that most of the contacts should be just that: a friendly contact only. No sales pitch.

But she also tested dropping each person a pre-holiday e-mail with a link to their online store, highlighting the special one-of-a-kind gift items. A small printed catalog went out in the spring featuring the new line, with editorial information to entice customers to come again to their area.

The results were good the first year. Among the many buyers was a businessman who had attracted many compliments on his silver belt buckle. He bought similar designs for two-dozen key customers.

A woman purchased earrings for several friends who, in turn, began shopping at their online store.

Helen sent a thank-you note by mail for every order.

Many who received birthday cards actually called or e-mailed to thank Helen and Larry for remembering them. As the new season approached, they compared the year-to-year sales and realized they were out of the danger zone.

When summer started and the tourists began arriving in town, many made Larry's store their first stop. The store was often crowded, as people would sit and talk with the couple like old friends. Helen took pictures of the customers with Larry and included them in the summer mailings.

By the second year, the momentum of the regular contacts had helped ease the seasonal ups and downs. Their quirky *Gazette*, a folksy newsletter, and the cards for birthdays and Christmas, helped them form lasting bonds with their customers and fans.

◆ ◆ ◆

In this chapter, you'll find sample plans for three main groups representing your five relationship circles:

▶ Customers and prospects

▶ Business colleagues and acquaintances

▶ Friends and family

These are suggestions only, to show you how you can put together your own Perpetual Contact System. Consider these guidelines as a place to start. But use your imagination.

Sample plan for customers and prospects.

By now, you've learned about many ways to stay in touch and you understand how keeping in contact in a friendly, non-intrusive way improves your chances of being the choice when it's time to buy or make a referral.

One that we haven't discussed is the newsletter. Many marketers are firm believers in newsletters, including Dan Kennedy, author/speaker/consultant.

He recommends a monthly newsletter. Why?

In *No B.S. Direct Marketing – The Ultimate No Holds Barred Kick Butt Take No Prisoners Direct Marketing for Non-Direct Marketing Businesses,* Dan advises. . .

"Real publications are monthly. . . You want it to arrive in your customers' mailboxes every month to say hi, bring some good cheer, deliver some useful tips and information, remind them you're ready to serve them, thank people for referrals, and make a special offer.

"After all, which month don't you want your customers coming back and making referrals?"

Many businesses find e-mailed newsletters to be highly effective and very affordable, although Kennedy's personal preference is for mailed newsletters.

Attractive HTML formats are available, but be aware some of the most popular e-mail newsletters are in plain text, often filled with links to information online.

There is no single right way to do an e-mail newsletter, but content is always the main focus.

Also, sending large quantities of e-mail through your own Internet provider can cause some real problems, including delays and the assumption that you're sending spam, among others.

There are a number of services you can use that not only let you avoid the annoying problems of sending bulk e-mails yourself, but also let you track how many people open your newsletter.

There is also software available. But do your research to get not only the most appropriate service or software, but also protection against being tagged a spammer.

Sending the newsletter to customers is obvious, but why send it to prospects? Since you will address customers in the copy, it can help prospects see you in action as you interact with customers. They can become more familiar with your products and services.

Also, as you tell customers about any exciting news – a product introduction or an article about your business in the media – your prospects get to learn about it as well.

Prospects' "buying cycle" often won't match your preferred "selling cycle." Keeping them engaged and informed can build trust and strengthen their confidence in buying from you. The newsletter lays a strong foundation for a year full of "touches."

Here's a sample of a basic 26-time contact plan, which includes two touches per month plus either a Thanksgiving or Christmas greeting. You'll add the birthday greeting wherever it falls in the year.

January
Newsletter
Festival of Sleep Day – holiday greeting (3rd)

February
Newsletter
Valentine's Day – holiday greeting (14th)

March
Newsletter
The Ides of March – holiday greeting (15th)

April
Newsletter
Hairstyle Appreciation Day – holiday greeting (30th)

May
Newsletter
Lost Sock Memorial Day – holiday greeting (9th)

June
Newsletter
E-mail Week – holiday greeting (2nd week)

July
Newsletter
Work-a-holics Day – holiday greeting (5th)

August
Newsletter
A perfect pair! National Picnic Month & Lazy Day –
  holiday greeting (10th)

September
Newsletter
Ask a Stupid Question Day – holiday greeting (28th)

October
Newsletter
Get Organized Week – holiday greeting (1st week)

November
Newsletter
Marooned Without a Compass Day – holiday greeting (6th)
Happy Thanksgiving – holiday greeting (an option to a
  Christmas card)

December
Newsletter
Christmas card – holiday greeting (optional if you
  send a Thanksgiving greeting)
National Bicarbonate of Soda Day – holiday greeting (30th)

Additional contacts with customers and prospects.

Here are suggestions for additional contacts that you can drop into your Perpetual Contact schedule as appropriate for your business:

▸ Quarterly cards, post cards or e-mails sent from trade shows or conferences ("Here we are at the XYZ Show. I've posted digital photos of our team and the new widgets we're evaluating at www.companysite.com.").

By sending messages from a business event, you're "taking them with you" and including customers and prospects in the action.

▸ Weekly e-mails: links, tips and quotes make good choices. Although we've focused on mailed contacts, small business owners are also using e-mails to link customers and prospects to video or audio tips hosted on their business sites.

Just be aware that open rates are dropping. Whatever you send must be pertinent and not just create more "noise" for the recipient.

▸ Twitter and other social networks are viable methods of building your profile and staying in front of potential customers and your customer base. However, building a real relationship takes a personal touch.

▸ Send an invitation for an educational teleseminar or Webinar. Make this a high-value event for your customers even if the purpose is to present an opportunity to purchase products or services.

For prospects, consider a live Q&A session to address the unknowns that could be in the way of making a buying decision.

▸ When you come across an article relevant to your customers and prospects, send a link with your brief comments of why you believe it's important for them.

▸ Review Chapter 8, "Thought you'd be interested in this," to find ideas to make one-to-one contacts relevant to specific individuals – not your whole list – whenever you can.

This list is a guideline. By all means adjust and adapt to suit your own business, industry, customers and prospects. The point is to make sure you intersperse personal, non-sales items with the marketing messages.

The One-Card-a-Day Plan

Some small business owners start out feeling that "a plan" is still too much for them to handle. Start with the easiest plan of all that takes just 60-seconds a day. Send a card each day to one individual on your list. It doesn't seem like much, but over a year, the impact can be significant.

It won't take long to prove to yourself the value of sending cards and staying in touch. It can be a birthday card, a "thinking of you" card or any one of the ideas outlined throughout this book.

The important thing is to get started. And to increase your impact with the cards, you can increase the number sent each day.

Each card sent means another relationship is stronger, the feelings are cordial, and you're top-of-mind. This is key to receiving ongoing, enthusiastic referrals.

Sample plan for business colleagues and acquaintances.

This group doesn't require relentless attention but, like a flower bed, it does need regular watering to keep you top-of-mind when someone asks for a recommendation for your type of goods or services. Within this group, you probably have some people who are closer than others. Adapt accordingly.

There are four frequencies of contact you can apply at will:

▶ **Weekly** – an option for your business colleagues, but too frequent for general acquaintances

▶ **Monthly** – the optimal frequency to develop warmth and rapport

- **Bi-monthly** – an acceptable frequency as long as each "touch" is memorable

- **Quarterly** – the minimum contact frequency to avoid the "Who is this guy?" reaction

Are these hard and fast rules? No. But you need a place to get started until thinking of meaningful messages and information becomes natural to you.

What to send? The suggestions below are to get you thinking.

Always send a birthday card. In addition to the messages you send to the entire group, use your imagination and the individuals' interests – to send personal notes periodically to those you want to cultivate and develop a closer relationship.

- **Weekly** touches for business colleagues can be links to useful sites, quotations or tips.

- **Monthly** contacts should be of the same type. For example, use the entire series of holiday greetings or off-beat holidays.

  For business contacts, you can also send your newsletter if you have topics of general business interest, not just material about your niche.

- **Bi-monthly** contact must be memorable. For business associates, consider timely content or topical articles. Comment on books or articles you've recently read. Write your own restaurant reviews in your hometown and when you travel. Report on crazy business travel stories if you fly or drive for business

  Whatever you send, make sure it reflects your personality. You want the recipients to get a growing sense of who you are, as you're getting to know them.

- **Quarterly** contact can take advantage of key holidays with a humorous twist. For business acquaintances, use any of the ideas for bi-monthly. For "civilians," opt for any message that is fun, uplifting, out-of-the-ordinary (weird news) or in the news.

Sample plan for friends & family.

This group is much easier to deal with because you know these individuals. Your messages don't have to be on a schedule, but should be on the radar. By that I mean, your inner circle should hear from you a couple of times a month at minimum.

Fortunately, you have the full range of communications options that will be useful for this group: phone, cell phone, text messaging, Twitter, phone, e-mail, and yes, greeting cards.

Kody Bateman of Send Out Cards talks about "promptings," those times when you think about getting in touch with someone. Unfortunately, the thought slips your mind and you often don't follow through.

Think what can happen if you take action when someone crosses your mind. "Hi, I love you," "How are you doing," and "Just thinking of you" are all reasons to get in touch. And these messages can mean so much to people.

For this group, the plan is to answer the promptings and make sure everyone is on – and stays on – your radar. Showing that you care – saying that you care – is the currency of relationships.

Summary. . .

▸ Chart out plans for each group of contacts so you have a road map for the year. Change and revise the plans, but plot them out so you get your messages out.

▸ Remember to integrate birthday cards, thank you's and other communications into your plan. Be memorable. By staying in touch regularly with people in your various groups, you'll already be a step ahead of most people. But make your contacts memorable and appropriate for each audience and individual.

INDEX

3753050

Made in the USA